Overcoming Life's 7 Common Tragedies

Opportunities for Discovering God

CHRIS BENGUHE

Paulist Press
New York/Mahwah, NJ

Cover design by Sharyn Banks
Book design by Lynn Else

Library of Congress Cataloging-in-Publication Data

Benguhe, Chris.
    Overcoming life's 7 common tragedies : opportunities for discovering God / Chris Benguhe.
        p. cm.
    Includes bibliographical references (p.   ).
    ISBN-13: 978-0-8091-4391-7 (alk. paper)
    1. Spirituality. 2. Christian life. 3. Opportunity. I. Title.
    BV4501.3.B454 2008
    248.8'6—dc22

                                                    2008005338

Published by Paulist Press
997 Macarthur Boulevard
Mahwah, New Jersey 07430

www.paulistpress.com

Printed and bound in the
United States of America

Contents

Thank God for problems—
They made me appreciate all the wonderful people I'm lucky
enough to love.
Most especially Mom and Dad,
the rest of my family,
the best friends any man could pray for—
and last, but definitely not least, my dear Carolann.

Preface

A book is the culmination of the author's research, hard work, inspiration, determination, and a little bit of luck. However, that does not mean that he or she just pulled those ideas out of thin air.

This book is not about me, or simply what I believe, as much as it is a collection of ideas, observations, realizations, and the applied, collected beliefs of those who have been through the worst to realize the best. It is their stories and experiences that have opened up my eyes over the course of my life and upon which I have based much of the conclusions that I have been inspired to arrive at in this book.

I wish to thank specifically Karen Smyers, Jim Nabors, Roy Rinard, Charles Prestwood, Alfredo Molina, Clay Ginglen, Bobby Schindler, and Jeny Deng, as well as Mindy, Suzanne, Holly, Rosemarie, Hai, Olivia, Jennifer, J. D. Doug, Gail, Alexis, and Robin.

They were all kind and patient enough to take the time and effort to tell me their stories and to explicitly allow me to share those stories with you and many others through this book as well as in many articles about them I have written over the years. They asked for nothing in return except the assurance that their knowledge might help to inspire and educate others as to the positive potential of life's seven most-common tragedies.

All of these people have made a great difference in the lives of others through the hopeful acceptance of their suffering, their difficulties, and their challenges and by acknowledging the potential of those events to inspire, educate, or lift up others to new heights and new perspectives on life and living.

None of them experienced this transformation by simply looking out for themselves and what they could gain. None of them were on some modern-day quest to become the world's richest, or most famous, or even the most enlightened. They simply wanted to find a way to be the best they could be and learn to respect themselves and others through it all—the good and the bad times. They all succeeded in one way or another.

Their experiences plus that of many others not mentioned are what led me to the ideas and the realizations upon which this book is based. Rather than simply stating those realizations, it seemed to be far more valuable to explain the process by which I came to them and share with you many of the stories that inspired them as tangible proof of the legitimacy of those beliefs and philosophies.

I wish to thank them all here once again and ask that you give them all the reverence, the respect, and the appreciation they deserve for giving me the right to tell their stories and to give you all a little glimpse into their lives, so that your life could be that much more fulfilled.

1

Ditching Pop Psychology, Perfectionism, and the Quick Fix

I had wanted simply to convey to the reader by way of concrete example that life holds a potential meaning under any conditions, even the most miserable ones. And I thought that if the point were demonstrated in a situation as extreme as that in a concentration camp, my book might gain a hearing. I therefore felt responsible for writing down what I had gone through, for I thought it might be helpful for people who are prone to despair.

Viktor Frankl, Jewish psychiatrist, Holocaust survivor, and author of *Man's Search for Meaning*

Tragedy and hardship actually give us the opportunity to experience the ultimate joy God intends for us. Contrary to popular belief, the secret road to finding joy is not ridding our life of problems but learning how to respond to difficult times and less-than-ideal circumstances by faithfully loving and respecting ourselves and others while enduring those hardships. Life is ultimately not about winning but about loving each other while

1

we are caught up in the midst of the absolutely unavoidable tribulation that is a part of life on this planet.

That is the secret treasure that lies at the heart of tough times and the positive potential beyond life's seven most-common tragedies.

Everywhere you look these days, the media is filled with stories of tragedy and calamity. From the personal challenges we all face every day to wholesale disasters like terrorist attacks, hurricanes, wars, famine, and disease; the list goes on and on. Troubled times have been part of humanity's experience since we were cast out of the proverbial Garden of Eden. Isn't the whole point of the story of the Garden of Eden, after all, is that life is and will always be difficult?

Contrary to trite popular philosophy, bad things won't stop happening, and problems will always be a part of life, regardless of how good you get at navigating yours. We can improve our lives and can do our best to keep the waters at bay. However, the bottom line is that life is no bed of roses, at least not one without the thorns.

Yet, so many of us spend our lives either trying to escape the unavoidable experiences or reeling from their effects, waiting to be free of suffering before we allow ourselves to be content. To make matters worse, self-help gurus promote this misbegotten thinking, filling our brains with fantasies of pain-free living and ways to make happiness happen.

What if happiness isn't supposed to be the *goal* that God intended for us but rather the *by-product,* the side-effect, of a life of worthwhile living, buried deep within the experiences of the ordeals themselves. What if without one, maybe we cannot have the other? What if God intends for the tragedies and difficulties of our lives to be the route to our ultimate joy? In that case, it would be ridiculous to spend our lives trying to rid ourselves of the ultimate source of our joy.

This is not a suggestion that we should purposely pursue problems or work to make our lives more difficult simply to do so. What if overcoming our ordeals is not actually as important as how we respond to our struggles? Then maybe true joy can only be achieved through the inevitable hardships in our lives and how we choose to respond to those traumatic situations.

Perhaps we don't need to "get real," as some pop psychologists and self-help slingers proclaim, because we already are real, and our problems are real too. In fact, some of them may never be solved. Not all of life's hurdles can be vaulted with slick talk and "pull yourself up by your bootstraps" prodding; some must simply be endured nobly with respect and faith in our God, our loved ones, and ourselves.

The secret treasure of tragedy is the core belief that life is not about getting over our problems, but instead about loving each other while we deal with problems in a constructive, hard-working manner. After all, Christ instructs us to love. He does not tell us to love only when times are good. He does not tell us to love so that we can make friends and influence people, and he does not tell us to love only those who can get us somewhere.

Christ never says life is about finding happiness here on earth—it is about creating joy and being a joyful beacon of his love. There is a big difference between spending your life searching for bliss and creating a lifestyle in which you build a joyful environment in your world. The first is all about wanting to be at a party, where everything is easy and feels good. The other is about wanting to create a loving atmosphere and world that may not always be ideal, but which is filled with opportunities to serve God and each other in a loving manner.

It is easy to forget this in the face of massive, worldwide consumer-marketing, promising us pleasure and convincing us that we deserve it. In a world that is very comfortable for most of us compared to our forefathers, we have come to expect success and even riches. Maybe God never intended it to be that way all the time. Perhaps life was supposed to be difficult. At the end of the day, the month, the year, and our lives, the joy is to look back and know that we did the right things, the hard things, with hope in our hearts and strength in our stride even when it was not easy.

Ironically, those who develop the perspective and willpower to reject the former philosophy will find great harmony and contentment even when hardship, obstacles, and tragedies come their way. Serenity, or peace of mind, is possible when we endure our obstacles and issues with conscientious daily intention, rather than goal-oriented opportunism. Be all you can be, work hard, love greatly, and stand as tall as you can through the endless storms that beat you down. Do it because it's the right thing to do, not because you believe you'll get a new car, a new house, a better spouse, or a new life because of it.

Life's truest reward is to know that we are manifesting God's will "on earth as it is in heaven," not that we are experiencing unbridled happiness all the time. Sure, good times are a blessing and one that we should appreciate. But we cannot become so obsessed with experiencing those good times that we become dysfunctional at the mere thought of tough times. We cannot become so traumatized by our problems that we shut down when they happen. Yet once again, ironically, when we do not base our happiness on achieving a problem-free life, problems indeed seem to be more easily overcome.

The "Loving Man" versus the "Überman"

If you think this understanding sounds unrealistic, impractical, or just downright less desirable than pursuing a life of bliss, then examine your faith a little more closely. If we believe in the mystery and majesty of Jesus Christ, then we must believe that the route to joy is through living the life of Christ as best as we can, regardless of the hardship it entails.

Christ never took the easy way out. He did not spend his life trying to maximize his potential for success or trying to develop a strategy for actualizing his greatness here on earth. Have you ever read anything about Christ ridding himself of "negative energy" by staying away from people who would "bring him down," or any of the other suggestions that ooze like diseased sap out of the mouths of a thousand different self-appointed, self-help, self-absorbed messiahs?

In my previous book, *Beyond Courage: The 9 Principles of Heroism*, I wrote about how one of the faults of modernism is its obsession with perfectionism and the ultimate belief that human beings can overcome anything and anyone if we simply craft ourselves into well-engineered, perfectly tuned machines. This view of life dismisses our imperfect nature and supplants our need for God with the potential of the human machine. Perfectionism places *us* as God. The twentieth-century philosopher Frederick Nietzsche spoke of the *überman,* or superman, that he believed we could all become. Adolf Hitler adapted Nietzsche's philosophy to support his own promotion of a master race of those supermen that could beat anyone in art, sports, and ultimately war.

Perfectionism is a dangerous, diseased, and deadly philosophy that distorts the nature and value of humanity and God. Our society is rife with wayward souls who want the good life, the best of everything, and are convinced that we can have it all. When the cruel realities of life slap some of us in the face and tell us otherwise, we are convinced it is our own inadequacy or failure that caused our less-than-perfect state. We then descend to an even worse state of being than we were in before we started striving for all that perfection in the first place. Now convinced that we are worthless because we cannot "be it all" and "have it all," we give up on striving at all. We envy and hate all those others who can and do achieve their goals.

Yet despite its errors and its dangers, this deadly philosophy is more popular than ever in our culture, so much that popular psychologists have made a fortune selling it to a desperate public.

Consider, for instance, many of the most popular books being published today; some of them are even best sellers. Their very titles connote that life is a game with winners and losers. (Would Christ have been a winner or a loser by their standards?) Or else these books connote that a wild "have it all" life is built on secrets unknown to the common person, but of course discovered by the author, who's willing to reveal them for the price of the book.

Many of the pop psychologists that write these books have lists of principles or actions to follow. Now, ignoring for a moment that any mortal could *know* these secrets, their nature perfectly exemplifies the danger of perfectionism. As opposed to the Ten Commandments, which we already have and which are all about how to treat others, *these* laws are all about the self and how to perfect it.

The pop "holders of the truth" say that the knowledge is there for those who seek it, that they have to use it the right way, and that only then will they reap the benefits of wealth, health, or love. These pop gurus are so wrapped up in winning this

"impossible-to-win" game that they miss the whole point of life—
to love. Jesus did not play by win-it-all rules, or by the rules of
the society that he came to liberate. If he had, today we would all
be pagan-worshipping subjects of the Roman Empire.

Perhaps the worst of these pop secrets is that the world
completely revolves around how *you* see it, not how your parents,
your boss, your family, or God sees it. Nobody else matters.
Reality is all about *you* and, in fact, you create your own experience, your own life. You create the actual situations you are in
and the emotions that flow from those situations. And if you
don't find yourself in good situations, well—somehow you blew
it. It's your fault, not the fault of these gurus with their absurd
obsession with a self-centered, self-created universe. As if we do
not already have enough problems teaching our children to sepa-
rate fiction from reality in this world of movies and entertainment-
based perception, now these false prophets want to tell us that
there is no reality at all.

The reality of Viktor Frankl, the man whose words opened
up this chapter, was formed during his internment in four concentration camps during World War II, where he watched his
wife, parents, and brother killed. Should he have been better at
controlling his emotions or creating his own reality? Not according to Frankl. In his existentialist masterpiece, *Man's Search for
Meaning,* he wrote, "We must never forget that we may also find
meaning in life when confronted with a hopeless situation, when
facing a fate that cannot be changed. For what then matters is to
bear witness to the uniquely human potential at its best, which is
to transform a personal tragedy into a triumph, to turn one's
predicament into a human achievement."[1] Frankl could not
escape or avoid the utter desolation of his situation, but he could
still see value in it.

For all of us, there is a reality, and no amount of positive thinking or perception-twisting rhetoric is going to make it go away. We can make that reality meaningful and constructive not by becoming obsessed with always changing it, but by finding a noble purpose in the way we deal with it, the way we respond to the millions of different criteria that are beyond our control. That purpose is to love and to be loved by others. Even if we fail, even if we cannot succeed at achieving our secondary desires, there should and can be a tremendous contentment in knowing that we will never fail at trying to endure even our so-called failure with dignity and love. Love is the real goal, and all the other good fortune is just icing on the cake.

Life Is Not a Game, So Stop Trying to Win It!

The most remarkably absurd thing about the whole self-centered view of the world is that it is actually contrary to serving the self in the long run because it is self-destructive. Since we can never achieve perfection (we will always fail at something), and since we will repeatedly encounter tough times and tragedies beyond our control, and at other times so tough that they overcome us, the delusion that we can deflect them all sets us up for a hard fall. Then when we do fail, we feel useless and even more worthless than we did before adopting the philosophy of perfectionism in the first place.

It is from that perspective that tragedy destroys us the most, because we believe that bad times are not supposed to happen, or that they are not supposed to hurt, or that we are all supposed to be able to vault over them like some kind of superhero.

However, on the other hand, if your core belief is that life is not about getting over our problems but instead about loving each other while we deal with problems in a constructive manner, then all of that changes. If you accept Christ's instruction to love, to create joy and to be a joyful beacon of his love as your ultimate and overriding goal, you suddenly become connected to an innate and ultimate force, one which can never mislead you as long as you keep working at loving others. And if you stop spending your life searching for bliss, and instead deriving your meaning and purpose from attempting to create a lifestyle in which you build a joyful, loving environment in your world, you can never be ultimately defeated and can never be destroyed.

This response to problems is a powerful antidote to the distressing headlines and the struggles we face everyday. It does not pretend that pain and problems don't exist in our world, but rather it encourages us to see the positive potential of life's most common catastrophes.

The following chapters consider what tragedy is and how it tries to prevent us from realizing our full potential. Steps that can help us to accept our plight in a positive manner will be examined. Some real-life situations and examples that have challenged and blessed others will also be considered.

2
The Tragedy Behind Seven Common Catastrophes

Never give in. Never, never, never, never in nothing great or small, large or petty, never give in except to convictions of honor and good sense, never yield to force; never yield to the apparently overwhelming might of the enemy.

Sir Winston Churchill, British Prime Minister
1940–45 and 1951–55

If life is not so much about getting over a tragedy as it is about enduring the tragedy nobly and finding meaning in it, is it possible to stop from getting mired in your problems, getting so bogged down in tragedy and depression that you give up trying to escape it? If allowed, tragedy can dominate and control your life absolutely.

When we get caught up in dwelling on a tragedy and being mired in the self-pity that it produces, it is really just another form of selfishness, one that threatens to destroy us and everyone around us. People sometimes become so caught up in their self-pity or their depression that they do not want to hear anything that is contrary. They actually can start deriving a certain pleasure from their pain, an ownership of it, like a badge of courage. Think about how many times you have in your own life, or have seen in others, the tendency to want to stay in a bad mood. That is a very minor example of *"Let's see how good at being miserable I can be."*

Once again, it is only by reaching outside of our individual problems that we can actually attain self-awareness, self-respect, and peace of mind. Rejecting our self-pity and our obsession with lack of self-satisfaction is the route to a positive effect on the world and ultimately back on ourselves.

Consider how just about every tragedy in this book gets worse when we focus on it and us. It is like driving a car or riding a bike. You will go in the direction that you are looking at. If you are focusing on the problem, the tragedy, the wrong direction, then that's where you will go. If you are focusing on the right direction, then that tends to be where you will go. The Catholic Catechism describes sin as "missing the mark." That is because we are not focused on God's direction but another direction of our own egotistical desire that sends us another way. We cannot aim in two different directions at once; we get nowhere.

Such is the case with tragedy. We cannot focus on the tragedy because then we are apt to gravitate toward it; but neither should we focus solely on the solution because then we will miss the whole point of life's goal of love. Both are what we want to dwell on; we are irresistibly and dangerously drawn to them like moths to a flame, the flame of our own selfish desire. When we focus only on the good life, the way we want things to be, we fall into all the pitfalls as described in the previous chapter. When we focus on the tragedy, the hardship, the obstacles, and the unhappiness we hate, then we fall into the same trap ironically in another way. In the first case, we are wrapped up only in our own desires for success. In the second case, we are focused on our potential capacity for sadness, corruption, evil, and malaise.

If we do not get driven into the self-help cycle, the "I am great" whirlpool, we can become drawn into the "woe is me" cycle. Either way we are obsessed with the self. Either way we get exactly what we are aiming for, a world of the self, which cuts us off from the common good, the common strength, and the common soul of humanity and God. Either way, when we make ourselves the center of our crumbling world, it is inevitable that the weight of that world is going to fall on us.

The fact that you are focusing on the problem, on the tragedy, and on the despair is opening you up to only half the experience that God has planned for you. Problems have a potential, and obstacles and tragedy may be the route by which we experience much of what God intends for us. In order for us to receive that knowledge, experience, and any of the gifts that God intends for us, we must follow the process through to its conclusion, enduring the tragedy nobly, with the intention God desires of us—love of God and love of neighbor. That is the line of reasoning that we should be following, not simply how to get over the problem.

Applying that directive clearly instructs us not to wallow in self-pity and possible demise but to learn from the situation, to savor the opportunities to love and to be loved. These situations provide ways to love and respect ourselves and others. It is ever-so-tempting to do the exact opposite.

It is similar to what happens with New Year's resolutions. We ring in each year with all kinds of good intentions for the year to come. To live a better life, work harder at our job, eat healthier, be a better friend, mate, parent, sibling, or whatever—the list goes on and on for all of us. Hopefully you do not come up with your resolution simply to revel in how great you can become or to marvel at your ability to transform; you really want to be a better person so you can add that much joy to your world and those that are in it.

However, how many of us commit to it? How often have you thrown in the towel on your new life because your plan did not work out quite as well as you had hoped? Then you beat yourself up and make everybody else around you suffer your self-pity, instead of continuing to work toward the common good by living the best life you can lead regardless of your occasional failures. That is missing the whole point, right?

In truth, you already have succeeded! You are the victor simply because you committed your strength and courage to try to make yourself and the world better. Whatever happiness and prosperity life has in store for you will definitely be found within that sincere struggle to improve your ability to love, even if it seems as if you are failing miserably to pull off your incidental goal, even if you are miserable while doing it. That means keep on trying after you break down and even when it appears as if your goal may be further off than ever.

It is so very tempting in the mechanized, technologically advanced world we live in today to view ourselves as either a success or a failure based on whether or not we have achieved our goals, instead of basing our self-esteem on the level and extent of our efforts. There is nothing more distracting to our attempts to live a better life and to be a better person than to get depressed or demoralized because we don't get exactly where we want to go at the precise moment that we all want to get there. We cannot let what may seem like setbacks deter us from the bigger picture of our decision to improve our daily efforts for the good of all.

Down deep, all that we do and learn on the road of life is so much more important than what we achieve when we get to wherever it is we find ourselves. When that road becomes a difficult one to travel, we learn the most important thing of all, that the reason for taking the trip in the first place is to contribute to the world around us while loving those whom we encounter along the way. As long as we are constantly trying to be better at that, we are a success.

Never stop heading in the right direction, even if it seems like your destination is a million miles away or if life's countless obstacles and catastrophes are threatening to distract you. Keep your eyes focused on the road ahead, not the perilous pitfalls, nor the sensational sights on the side of the road. You are not alone on this journey, and the rest of the world really appreciates you doing your share of the driving as we all head toward a better world and a better life.

You Endure Because the World Needs You To!

That sentiment perfectly echoes the words of Winston Churchill that began this chapter. He was the great British military leader and political icon that led Britain during World War II and beyond. Churchill was a man who, for all his faults, never relented against all odds in the fight for his nation. As Adolf Hitler's Nazi empire tried to take over the world, Churchill inspired his tiny island-nation to stand firm despite merciless bombardment day in and day out for years while he worked furiously to convince the rest of the world to come to his aid. He was a man who made many miracles happen because of his faith and his fortitude. With simple but powerful words, and the spirit that they inspired, Churchill most assuredly saved the free world from evil and tyranny because of his refusal to give up trying, despite the barely defensive effort his nation could muster. The effort itself made a difference, a big difference that convinced others to take up the fight.

Two thousand years before Churchill, another man who refused to give up came our way to save the world as well. He spoke similar words in a different way. This man came with a message of love, truth, and purity in his heart. He spoke of being all that our Father intended for us, the best we could be to each other. That man was Jesus Christ. Time after time, he exhibited the power of perseverance in the face of tragedy as many tried in vain to defeat him and his message. He refused to falter, and he refused to change his course or to diverge from his tragic end and the lifestyle he proclaimed to be "the way" to salvation when he was tempted to do so by his own fears, weakness, and doubt. Not even the pains of crucifixion and the punishment of death made him give up or give in to the pressure to deny his Father's will.

It is the same with tragedy and hardship for all of us. We must endure, not to lament, but to resist the world's attempts to distract us from the life that God wants us to lead, the good and inspired life that ultimately and cumulatively results in the greatest good for all, regardless of the pains and costs associated with doing that.

What Are Seven of the Most Common Tragedies?

1. Job Blues

"By the sweat of your face you shall eat bread until you return to the ground, for out of it you were taken," states Genesis

3:19. Hard work is the way that we shall support ourselves. Yet, we are often disgruntled with our mission to work hard. We even go so far as to believe that we must be perpetually excited and entertained by that mission, otherwise we must be on the wrong track in life.

Life was not intended to be easy, nor was it intended to be entirely pleasurable. Hollywood, Madison Avenue marketers, and the media have filled our heads with visions of splendor and easy living, so much so that we think we cannot possibly bear to work too hard or tolerate a job that does not perfectly fit our understanding for that single moment of our lives. The result is an ever-present lack of contentment with our workplace responsibilities.

Now this is in no way a criticism of society's inability to persevere. On the contrary, we can and will persevere only if we stop looking at our inevitable day-to-day struggle as some kind of failure and instead see it as an integral opportunity to contribute and do our part.

If we take a moment to think about our *duty* to help others and to look at work as an opportunity to do that duty, then suddenly we are imbued with a tremendous ability to get up every morning and toil responsibly.

2. Breakups, Divorce, and Loneliness

Everyone knows the horrible pain and suffering that accompany the breakup of a relationship, whether it is the sadness that comes at the end of a long-term relationship or the horrible life-altering destruction that occurs when a divorce tears lives and families apart.

It is during these times, when despair, loneliness, and depression leave us asking "Why bother?" that we must learn to look beyond the blame and the pain and into our integral need to respect ourselves and others as God intends us to within a mutually respectful relationship.

The lesson is that the way to meet the right person is by *being* the right person yourself and shining like a beacon to the rest of the world, so all those potentially right people can see you all the more clearly, and then by pursuing a relationship that allows you to continue to shine. If we work hard, do what we were put here on this earth to do, and make our lives an example of love and respect for others, we will be led in the right direction, and other respectful, faithful people will be led to us.

Furthermore, bad relationships can inspire us to ask: Was this relationship taking us in the wrong direction? Or was it a self-abusive or codependent relationship? If so, is our desire to maintain it going to fly in the face of what God really wants for us? If, on the other hand, the relationship was a blessed and consecrated one that was truly meant for us, then an end can simply be a wake-up call to work on respect and to inspire others to respect us and God.

Whatever the case, the answer to our confusion and our pain is beyond the tragedy of the breakup itself. We will find it within the development of our ability to make it through such events with dignity and love in our hearts for all. If we do so, then we will be putting our best foot forward toward a better view of the tragedy of separation.

Reach out in your everyday life and live the life God wants you to. Open your heart to those the Lord sends your way while you are doing his work. Then be patient. To us, it may seem like God isn't always on time, but he is always on target!

3. Illness

A tough tragedy to endure is that of serious illness, especially when it's long-term. Illness robs the body, the mind, and the soul of the healthy nourishment and fortification needed for life. This is probably why Jesus spent such a considerable amount of his life curing the sick and why the anointing of the sick is important enough to be one of the blessed sacraments. Do we spend so much time fearing, lamenting, and disparaging illness in our society that we overlook its possible purpose and its value—spiritually, psychologically, and even physically?

Pope John Paul II was criticized for refusing to pass the torch in light of his progressive illness. The reason for his decision, most believe, was that he wished to demonstrate the value of the experience of illness, as well as to uphold the dignity of suffering illness in a world that has become less and less tolerant of human imperfection. Beyond the tragedy of illness is the unique experience for reflection and the opportunity to uphold our dignity, which exists in all circumstances.

What is the purpose of illness? Is there a wisdom that comes when we are forced to accept our physical weakness and vulnerability, while simultaneously learning how to transcend our physical being and situation to reach a higher plane of existence and realization? If so, the spiritual reward could be greater than imaginable as we find a spiritual clarity in the physical confusion of our malfunctioning bodies. As we force ourselves to dispel our bitterness and learn how to love while in our physically depleted state, we become a true fountainhead of God's pure love.

4. Money Trouble

Did you know that lottery winners have one of the highest per-capita incidences of bankruptcy of any single demographic group in the United States? After they have won the money, many believed it would put them on easy street. Just tune in to VH1's *Where Are They Now* and its hit parade of former pop stars for many other examples of those who had it all and lost it only to wind up on skid row.

"It's not whether you win or lose, but how you play the game" is an all-too-familiar adage that may seem anachronistic nowadays in the world of the rampant consumerist materialism that surrounds us. Although we all certainly need to pay our own way and put a roof over our heads, the need to tighten our belts could sometimes be a good thing. Perhaps we all don't need as much as we think, or have been convinced, that we need.

As the demands of modern living and the emphasis on material success grow, so does the preoccupation with winning that gets us so obsessed with worldly success that we forget about succeeding in God's eyes by doing the right thing and enriching our souls and the souls of others.

Sometimes when we lose some of those riches and get that material clutter out of our hearts and souls, we can see God and his way a little clearer. Losing a little may actually be your route to gaining a lot. Transform your perspective on financial woes, and you may turn your tribulation into contemplation and appreciation.

You do not have to be poor to be happy nor should you deliberately try to lose it all. If we let the desire for more money dominate our lives, then the lack of it convinces us that we are lost. Christ actually instructed his apostles to give up all their money and their possessions. Why? Is it because money is evil? No, but when the Bible says it is the "root" of evil, it clearly means that something can happen within us that leads us to evil when we are dealing with it. So not having enough of it may just lead us in the right direction after all.

5. Family Trouble

God endows all people with free will and the right to exercise that free will. Sometimes they make the wrong choice and do the wrong thing. They stray outside the family of God, and sometimes they become mean and annoying to others. None of us has the right to take away their choice to do the wrong thing. That is the key to understanding and tolerating family skirmishes.

Inevitably, even when nobody is really to blame, our families and friends sometimes get on our nerves or hurt our feelings because of their actions or inaction. So we try to get them to stop doing whatever they are doing and to shape up to our liking. Since we are so close to them, we assume more of a right to alter their behavior than we would with a stranger.

As annoying as those times may seem, they are there to teach us to stop trying to play God. We cannot make people into our own image, and we cannot treat people like machines that either work "right" or are disposable. Difficulties and squabbles over the foibles of our loved ones can remind us of this fact.

Even more important, they make us find a better way of dealing with those difficulties to reap God's love. When strife and struggle threaten to tear a family apart, we must step up to the plate and be the best we can be, so they can see by example how they should act without us preaching or trying to change them directly. Family is the greatest representation of God's will on earth, for it prods us to love unconditionally. God implores us over and over again in the Bible to have a higher tolerance with family, to endure more and demand less, and to love despite weakness, flaws, and problems.

In the most extreme cases of abuse, neglect, and criminal endangerment by a family member, there is a time when we must protect ourselves or others. Doing so may in fact require that we distance ourselves from the perpetrator. Even in these extremes, while protecting our autonomy, we may find great wisdom and peace in acknowledging our family, with all their flaws.

6. Death

Why must people die? This question has surely been asked since the first human being took his last breath. Even in this advanced age where life expectancy continues to reach new heights, there is still no escaping the pain and suffering that accompanies the death of a loved one or the impending fear of one's own demise. However, we can realize a new perspective on such events that allows us to focus on others instead of our own pain.

Ever since I was a child and attended my first funeral, I was amazed by how many of my relatives and family friends were present, people I had not seen in years, people I probably should have seen more often. The same seems to be true about every funeral that one attends.

When God calls one of us home to be in his presence, he most surely has a reason, even if it is beyond our comprehension. However, what is relevant to us is our ability to use this experience to love and support those who gather together in this time of tragedy and to recognize and appreciate the love others bring our way that we otherwise may not have experienced.

We can use that love to bolster others and to make the world a better place. We can transform that love and tenderness into fuel for life and become someone with a better view. Then death will not just be a tragedy but a triumph for God's love as it spreads life through death.

7. Bad Choices, Dead Ends, and Giving Up!

Sex, booze, drugs, crime—the world is littered with behavioral maladies. People make mistakes, and from time to time any one of us can find ourselves heading down the wrong path. That is to be expected. However, what is worse is that we don't see our weakness as an opportunity and a call to humble ourselves to God and his love. We choose instead to go it alone, isolating ourselves in our struggle, or we refuse to see the failure in our lives as a sign of misdirection.

Addictions, destructive behaviors, general confusion, or loss of direction in our lives may actually be our opportunity to gain greater insight into God's direction. God works in mysterious ways, usually through his other children. That means that humbling ourselves to a loved one in order to ask for a helping hand out of our dilemma may be the route that moves us closer to him and our own purpose.

Think about this for a moment. If you were God and gave people free will, then you needed to let them make their own decisions and lead their own lives just like a parent must with an adult child. Yet, you still wanted to help them, you still wanted to lead them. You loved them so much that you still wanted them to make the right decisions. How would you do it? Well, not supposing for a moment that I know what God thinks, let me propose that if the Creator designed a world that would not work for us when we headed in the wrong direction, then it would be a great way to redirect us.

God sends us people for a reason, but just as we must come to God without pride, it takes humility to ask those we love, and those who love us, for help. Then we allow God to work in their hearts to help us. Their hearts become like a giant magnifying glass concentrating God's love into a powerful ray and that light spreads far beyond our problems or mishaps to light up the world.

Instead of seeing our own failures, we can see God's way of affirming his light and presence in the world and to attract more and more followers to his illuminated way. When we reject that love or refuse to kneel in its awesome presence by egomaniacally thinking more about our downfall than about the opportunity to let God do his thing in our lives through that hardship, then we are rejecting God's love and the grace it brings.

As natural as the desire to end our own mess might seem, it is really another form of egoism and self-centeredness. When life goes wrong, or we go wrong, we must realize that our "failure" is a tremendous opportunity to let God into our lives by searching our souls and by letting others help. Failure is so often the best way for God to send the love of others into our lives and to destroy our sinful egoism in order to open our hearts to the help that is needed to receive all the glory of his love.

3
Seven Steps to Serenity

Given that tragedy can possibly be the conduit to a better understanding of life as well as a more contented existence, how do we put that into action?

I have observed seven steps in people who have made positive transitions from tragedy that can help prevent the rest of us from reacting negatively to tragedy and lead us to responding positively to what we must realize are normal life events.

STEP 1. Avoid the Tragedy Spiral

Why do all public doors open outward instead of inward? It is because of the tragic tale of the Hollywood Coconut Grove over a half a century ago. After a small fire erupted, people panicked. As they frantically tried to escape the growing fire, they trampled each other, turning a fire into a deadly stampede. Finally, the throng of frenzied patrons crammed up against the doors so tightly that nobody could open them. The panic from the original tragedy spiraled out of control into a catastrophe of the highest order, just like it does so many times in life. It is often difficult to resist the temptation to panic, which results in worse circumstances than those with which we began.

The following is a good example. A young soldier was in the hospital recovering from knee surgery. He's been deserted by his wife who cleared out his bank account as her parting gesture. She left him with their three-year-old child and no money to feed him because she even had his checks forwarded to her new address. Trying to resolve this dilemma became a legal nightmare.

Instead of staying calm and weathering the storm, he panicked and decided to rob an old man's house after he heard there was a sizeable amount of cash in the man's closet. He was caught in the act, shots were exchanged, and the owner of the house was left dead. Within a month Corporal Billy Moore was in jail awaiting execution for his crime. A tragedy turned into a catastrophe all because of the tragedy spiral. It took sixteen years for Moore to reverse his fortunes, narrowly avoiding execution through a series of miraculous events that came about after completely reexamining his series of tragedies and restructuring the way he looked at his life, which is what prompted me to interview him.

How many times have you or someone you know spiraled out of control into a systemic breakdown because of a single terrible event? For instance, a romantic breakup leads to a drinking binge to a DUI to a lost job to a lost life. Someone overreacts to getting cut off on the freeway, so they retaliate by cutting their antagonist off, inadvertently forcing them to crash into a school bus filled with children. Financial ups and downs may be dealt with by gambling, which often leads to catastrophic financial troubles far worse than the ones an individual was trying to escape. There is no end to how low the tragedy spiral can take you if you don't put the brakes on before you lose everything. It all starts with a single tragic event.

We must realize we have no control over whether or not many of tragic events occur, but we can choose to respond to those events calmly and responsibly, so that we do not fall into the *tragedy spiral,* a slippery slope of negative behavior leading to more catastrophes.

One should not avoid, ignore, or pretend that your tragedy did not happen or that it did not matter. Quite contrarily, the positive potential of your future may actually lie deep within an understanding of the tragedy itself: why it happened, how it happened, and how to deal with it. As far as Step 1 is concerned, the important thing to remember is to put the brakes on.

There used to be a public service announcement years ago with Dick Van Dyke informing viewers of what to do in case of a fire. "Stop! Drop! And Roll!" was advised in case you were ever trapped in a smoke-filled room. That is the perfect advice when a tragedy happens in your life. Don't panic! *Stop* whatever you are doing because it obviously has either led to or is leading to some kind of tragedy. Then *drop* the attitude and the pain that you are letting dominate your disposition. Finally, *roll* with the punches, so to speak.

Remember, this is not the end of the world, but the beginning of your journey to understand the meaning and the positive potential of the catastrophe that just happened. Act responsibly and lovingly just like you would under any normal circumstances. Do not let the extremes make you an extremist. Stick to the plan and do not get caught in the tragedy spiral.

STEP 2. Reality Check

Seeing the positive potential in tragedy is not about adopting some unrealistic rosy perspective on life, or some power approach that says you are the master of your universe. It is about simply freeing yourself from the opposite: the denial that anything good can come from bad, and the obsession with the negative that many of us fall into after a tragedy. It can be explained very well with a new take on the old "glass is half-empty or half-full analogy." What happens when the glass is actually completely empty? That is when the positive realist admits that the glass is empty, but figures out that the glass itself is worth something. It may be a family heirloom or perhaps it can be used for something else even better than holding water. Another way to consider this is to see it as the seat of your soul, your purpose, and your potential worth and meaning.

In realistic terms, get over the horror of the tragedy and start examining all the possible ramifications of the event, both positive and negative. It is more than just counting your blessings; it is looking deeper to find out what they are. There could be something you can learn about yourself or about others buried in the tragedy. There could be a long-overlooked option or opportunity for some better life or better course of action there. There could be a lifesaving stop to an activity that would have caused much more pain or damage in the long run. Finally, there almost always is the potential for tomorrow to be better than today, if you are willing to stop focusing on the tragedy itself.

A woman on a city bus in New York was overwrought with sadness after losing her job, her fiancé, her apartment, and her car all on the same day. As she sat pondering the seeming meaninglessness of her misfortune and shedding a tear or two, a man in the back of the bus penned her a brief note. He secretly slipped the note into her bag as she passed him to get off the bus. When she arrived at home later, she found the mysterious note and read it.

He explained to her that he had been diagnosed with terminal cancer a few weeks back and had just returned to the hospital for the results of some follow-up tests earlier that day. First, he took a long walk in nearby Central Park. There he enjoyed the sound of the birds chirping, the sight of children playing, and the joy of exchanging smiles with the people he passed along the way. He decided at that moment that as long as he was alive he would use that time to love life and love others, even if the tests confirmed he was dying of cancer. Amazingly, a few hours later when he received those test results, he learned that the cancer was inexplicably gone.

As the young girl read the note from the man she barely even noticed on the bus, she suddenly was overcome with joy. She put away her self-pity and called a good friend to tell her how lucky she was to be alive. Years later that woman on the bus rose to be the very successful CEO of a Manhattan company who garnered national recognition for creating corporate programs aimed at helping her employees integrate achievement at work with a happy home-life, plus days off to help community-based charities. The reality of the tragic situation was that she had been given an opportunity to find a better job—and a better boyfriend who would not desert her during difficult times and circumstances.

This story helps illustrate how positive potential with an individual can lead to a more thorough and deeper understanding of the reality of the event. You need to change your perspective in order to reveal all those potentials. You must become realistic instead of pessimistic.

STEP 3. Be Loved

People make mistakes. From time to time, we all can find ourselves heading down the wrong path. However, what is worse is what happens when, rather than humbling ourselves to a loved one in order to ask for a helping hand out of our dilemma, we choose to refuse help and instead to isolate ourselves in our struggle, determined to resolve and fix the problems ourselves.

Even though we may convince ourselves it is nobler to right our wrongs on our own, are we actually alienating ourselves from God in prideful obstinacy by doing so? We become convinced that nobody else is smart enough or capable enough to play a part in our lives. We are in control and there is no way we are giving up any of that control to anyone else.

As the old saying goes, "It's lonely at the top." When we set ourselves up as top dog in our own lives so that nobody else can ever help direct us, it leads to incredible isolation. Not only does that isolation cut us off from God's wisdom and love as expressed through others, it also often results in greater tragedy or hardship for others.

As admirable as the desire to fix our own mess by ourselves might seem on the surface level, it is essentially another form of self-centeredness and egoism. Much of the time we cause more pain, suffering, and hurt to ourselves and to others than we would have if we just asked for and accepted help from someone who loved us in the first place.

A single mother of three had fallen deeper and deeper into the despair of alcoholism until finally the addiction ruined her life and threatened her very ability to care for her children. Rather than ask for help from her parents, who, she later realized, would have gladly helped her and rejoiced in the opportunity if only she told them of her struggle, she chose to keep her dereliction a secret until it landed her in jail for drunk driving. Then the very lives and welfare of her children were in jeopardy when the courts took custody of them away from her. Hearing the news not from her daughter but from the child protective-services department, her mother was heartbroken and emotionally devastated, not by her daughter's alcoholism or legal troubles but because she could not fathom how her own daughter never trusted her enough to come to her for help. This, in turn, made her feel as if she was an inadequate mother. The blow to her heart sent her to the hospital, where she died, quite literally, of a broken heart. Her daughter did not love her mother enough to trust her with the truth, and more important, she didn't let her mother do the one thing that most mothers live for—to love and to help their children.

God sends us people for a reason, but just as we are required to come to God without pride, it takes humility to ask those we love for help when we have gone astray or when we are in trouble. Then we must have the courage and conviction to humble ourselves and accept their help and direction. Only then can we allow God to work in their hearts to help us. Their hearts become like a giant magnifying glass concentrating God's love into a powerful ray that truly does light up the world like a huge flood-lamp for all to see that much more clearly by. The result goes so far beyond us and our problems or mishaps. That light acts as a powerful proof of God's love to them and to many other onlookers.

So, as we said before, by letting others help us, we help God to affirm his presence and attract more and more followers to his illuminated way. When we reject that love or refuse to kneel in its awesome presence, we are rejecting God's love and all the grace it brings. We then shut down that heavenly light.

Instead of being so ashamed of our wrongful ways that we reject God's love and the love of others, do just the opposite. Open your heart and head to the idea that your mistake is all part of God's plan to lead you into the arms of others and into the cradle of His love.

STEP 4. Be Loving

A twenty-one-year-old world-champion equestrian dove into a river and hit a hidden tree stump, breaking his neck. He was pulled out of the river dead and was miraculously resuscitated. He was told he would be paralyzed for life, and worse still, he would never speak again because of brain damage that occurred while he was not breathing. His father spent years working tirelessly to keep his son alive and to help him communicate with the outside world, devoting his life to him and hardly sleeping more than three hours a night. After seventeen years, his son woke up one day and spoke for the first time. His first words: "I love you, Dad." When I asked the father how he put up with such pain for so long, he said he was happy to have the opportunity to love his son more than most fathers ever have.

God is with us in tragedy just as much as he is with us in time of triumph, and he stands by us in times of solace and slumber just as he is with us in times of celebration. He does so by reminding us of what we were created to do—love each other. The ability to love is what we are designed for, so of course when we act according to that design, we are most content. Everything that we do in our lives is really just to effect that end. Whether it is working hard, looking good, becoming successful, or becoming rich, at its heart it is all an attempt to be able to love and be loved. That should inspire us through every hardship, from the death of a loved one to the death of relationships to job blues to joblessness and everything in between; to stand tall fighting the good fight with love and respect for ourselves and others first and foremost in our hearts.

How do we take such intellectual realities and integrate them practically into action? First of all, we must ask ourselves if we see our lives as one giant opportunity to derive our happiness from loving and respecting each other, as God designed us to. Or do we frequently fall victim to a more egocentric and arrogant view of life, wanting to fill our time with personal victories, looking to accumulate material goods, endlessly striving for our own simple, selfish wishes, and being disappointed when we don't get our way. If that is our ultimate desire, we will most assuredly be endlessly disappointed, since we always want more, better, and greater success.

Worldly pleasures and possessions are fine if they are realized to be gifts we get in order that we may share them with those we love. The focus must be on why we want them, how we get them, and how we use them to care for those we love.

Christ tells us over and over again in the New Testament to love our neighbors as ourselves. We were created to love and be loved, so acting according to our design by loving others and accepting love, even in times of pain and suffering, is the only thing that will bring us happiness. God gives us countless opportunities to do that in the very midst of our hardships and ordeals.

Love is practical, and it really does bring joy to the world. That means that this whole love concept is not only about loving others, but also about how all that love comes back to fill up our hearts with joy and happiness.

When you are down and out, do not isolate yourself in your self-pity and pain. Open your heart and your head to others and be as loving as you can be. Get up and help someone or say a kind word, when all you really feel like doing is complaining and lamenting.

Remember the tragic story of Corporal Billy Moore at the beginning of this chapter. After this man spent over sixteen years on death row, he became one of the only confessed and convicted killers to be released from jail because he had turned his life around to such a dramatic degree while behind bars. After turning his heart over to Christ and becoming an ordained minister behind bars, he began ministering to inmates to help change their hardened hearts. His efforts helped to end riots and foil murder plots at considerable risk to his own life. He helped to start a welfare program for indigent inmates so they could have basics such as books and games to pass the time while waiting to die, since nothing is given to death-row inmates. He began writing hundreds of letters a month to families outside of prison who asked for guidance and help with their own children or relatives who were trapped in a life of crime. He wrote extensively of his conversion, inspiring many outside of the walls of his prison to better their lives. Only moments before his scheduled execution, Billy Moore's sentence was permanently commuted. He was released from prison a year later.

To help you with Steps 3 and 4, the following "Road Map to Happiness" offers five simple questions that will remind you how important our relationships with each other really are, as well as the joy we derive from them.

Anytime you start to feel down, jot down the answers to these five simple questions.

Road Map to Happiness

- Who do you love (pick one person) and why are they so special to you?
- What's the nicest thing anybody ever did for you and how did it inspire or help you?
- What's the kindest thing you ever did for anybody else that helped to make their day or their life better? How has helping that person enhanced your own life?

- What is something positive that you saw somebody else do yesterday or today to help someone else, something which filled your heart with happiness? It could be a family member, a friend, or even a complete stranger who made somebody happy.
- Who loves you and how do they show it? How has their love changed your life?

STEP 5. Love Yourself!

Do you realize how much the world desperately needs you? Do you realize how crucial you are? *You* are an indispensable part of the world since God created you.

Logically, if you believe that human life is sacred, then you believe that your human life is just as sacred. So abusing or disrespecting yourself is ideologically just as immoral and destructive to the world's collective of love as doing so to another.

Few people realize just how easy it is to get caught up in a dangerous pattern of self-abusive or self-destructive behavior, which stems from forgetting to love and respect yourself and results in great human pain and suffering for society. Have you ever been married to or involved with someone with very low self-esteem or an individual caught up in self-destructive behavior? Were they a kind and supportive fountainhead of love and kindness helping the world every day? Or were they bitter, jealous, or possessive, suspecting the worst of you and abusing you in return for your affections?

Or consider disciplinary problems with your children. How many times do their behavior problems turn out to be the rebellious results of a child suffering feelings of worthlessness because of peer pressure or perceived physical, intellectual, or social inadequacies?

Criminals and addicts of all types were often brought up being told they were only capable of the minimum in life, thus suffering from low self-image long before they began their lives of despair. This led them to believe that such limited lives were all they deserved. Since they are worthless, it means humanity is worthless, which allows them to hurt and abuse others.

Napoleon, Hitler, and serial killers like Charles Manson all struggled at young ages with a bad self-image, which caused them to hate themselves. Their insecurities and feelings of worthlessness translated into inferior perspectives on human worth in general.

Maybe it is a matter of constantly reminding each other that we were divinely created and endowed with a divine mission, and that is what makes you and me important. Do not let anyone, yourself included, disrespect that sacred humanity.

That means so much more than just accepting and realizing your value; it means protecting and honoring that value by never engaging in self-abusive behavior. If you realize that loving and respecting yourself is just as important as loving others, you will not be led astray into believing that it is somehow noble or worthy to hurt yourself to help someone else. The biblical call for self-sacrifice does not equate to self-abuse or self-deprecation.

Remind yourself that Christ does not say that we should love others more than ourselves, but he says to love your neighbor "as" yourself. Logically, that means we should love ourselves as our neighbor. We must respect all human life, including our own.

STEP 6. Do the Legwork

A priest who was counseling me when I was going through a rough time gave me some of the simplest yet best advice I have ever been given: *Do the legwork and don't overanalyze.*

After working through all the ideas in Steps 1–5 comes the really challenging part: applying it in all the traumatic situations that come up in your life, regardless of how tempting it might be to sit back and dwell on the details of your catastrophe. It comes time to put one emotional foot in front of the other, never stopping to doubt your direction. If you do that, then you absolutely will get to where you are going—that is, finding the positive potential of life's most common catastrophes. If you continue to question and doubt your direction, always assuming the worst instead of the best, pushing away love instead of accepting it, hating yourself despite God's promise that you are worthy and important—then you will most surely stop dead in your tracks. So, you must simply do the legwork.

That means even when you are at the end of your rope, when you think all is bleak, when you think that you can't move forward in spite of all the intellectual, logical, and emotional proof that the first five steps have provided. You must believe that if you do all these things, that God will deliver you to the promised land. This brings us up to the last of the seven steps.

STEP 7. Keep the Faith

Christ's amazing dominion over death extends into every aspect of our existence, and it summons us to be hopeful and positive proofs of his almighty power and love. It is our honor and mission to be his beacons, never dimming under the shadows of life's turmoil.

By overcoming physical death, Jesus showed us all that through his example and faith in his father, every one of us can conquer the many forms of death, beyond the physical, that threaten to darken our lives and extinguish our light.

That means that through Christ we can overcome or endure everything and anything that comes our way. We must believe it to be true. His death and resurrection made eternal happiness and life after death possible for every one of us who follows and accepts his truth. Through Christ we also have the power to rise metaphorically during life from the mire of all the temporal destruction and death that threaten to kill our souls in this world as we prepare for our eternity in the next.

By accepting the pure love of our Lord and agreeing to spread that love, we will be granted the amazing power of resurrection every day of our life. If we accept the Lord's love and mission, then we are no longer slaves to our own weakness, our own pain and suffering, our own errors and sins, our own experiences and senses. We will no longer be overcome by the mayhem the world sends our way.

Remember that the Lord's Prayer says, "Thy kingdom come, thy will be done, on earth as it is in heaven." The life-giving power of the Lord is alive and well in this world, and we can receive and experience it every day, but we must open our heads and our hearts to it. It is ultimately a leap of faith that a life of values, morality, and intention of growing and spreading love and respect is the route to the greatest good and the greatest joy for all.

Prayer is an essential part of doing that and therefore should be part of our daily life. Truly having faith is about using all the talents God gave us to make the right decisions. After we have exhausted all of our gray matter on the subject, then it is time to let our hearts speak the will of our Lord, receiving his messages through prayer. Without that final element to our decision-making process on items of import, we are really not utilizing our Christian soul to its full extent and not availing ourselves to Christ to be his agents.

We need to pray each day for that guidance, strength, and support, so that we can make the right decisions in the Body of Christ. Then we must have the courage to listen to our hearts for the answer and to keep the faith and go with God!

Applying the Seven Steps of Serenity to Seven of the Most Common Catastrophes

Let us now look at each one of life's most common catastrophes from a new perspective. The easiest way to do that is to run through these seven steps in every catastrophic situation and working through that process, one catastrophe at a time.

In the following chapters, you will find anecdotal examples of those who were experiencing all the horror that catastrophe could bring their way. Often, they were mired in the tragedy spiral, allowing everything in their life to be ruined, their positive potential obscured by the rippling effects and affectations of a single catastrophe.

Then we will follow their lives as they learned the lessons of the positive attributes of catastrophes that helped them to find their way back to a meaningful life, a better view of the positive potential of life's seven most common catastrophes.

4
The Never-Work-Again Scam
Job Blues

Do you hate your job? Do you wonder why you have to work?
Does it upset you that others have better jobs or make more
money than you do? Are you confused about what you should do
for a living and feel lost and purposeless? Or have you recently
lost your job, either because you were fired or laid off, and you
feel your life is over because of it?

Have you ever considered that all of those problems, frus-
trations, and obstacles can motivate and inspire you? In general,
our unhappiness usually has a reason. Finding it or figuring out
a healthy way to confront it leads us to a greater understanding
of ourselves, of what we want, and of what we need.

The process of learning how to love and wage a career
simultaneously is a perfect starting point for seeing all of the
other catastrophes as potentially positive experiences. Trouble at
and with work is one of the easiest experiences to tolerate since
most of us are forced to work; avoiding it is not an option, so we
already have an incentive to deal with it.

Work's Greatest Reward

One day a man came upon the cocoon of a butterfly. Soon he noticed a small opening appear, and he sat and watched for several hours while the butterfly struggled to force its body through that little hole.

When it seemed to stop making progress, the man decided to help the butterfly, so he took a pair of scissors and snipped off the remaining bit of the cocoon.

The butterfly then emerged easily but it had a swollen body and small, shriveled wings. The man expected the wings would enlarge and expand to be able to support the body in time. Neither happened! The butterfly spent the rest of its life crawling around with a swollen body and shriveled wings, and it was never able to fly.

The man did not understand that the butterfly's struggle to get through the tiny opening was God's way of forcing fluid from the body of the butterfly into its wings, thus enabling the wings to mature so that it could fly when it achieved its freedom from the cocoon.

For many of us, our jobs are far more than just the way we make a living. They represent an important part of our identity and our growth. They help us support ourselves and support our loved ones. They allow us to prosper, to inspire us to reach higher, do more, contribute to society, and be a part of something more important than ourselves.

When things go wrong with our jobs, it is easy to see how it can threaten to destroy us emotionally and spiritually if we let it. Jobs are so important to us, so it is understandable that struggles associated with them sometimes seem unbearable. Whether it is tolerating the daily grind and trouble at work, losing a job, or never finding that perfect job we are all seeking, job dissatisfaction can be a whole lot more than an occupational hazard. It can threaten to destroy our livelihood, our families, and our souls.

Maybe the struggles of work are just God's way of helping us to mature and grow into the butterflies that we all one day hope, and are intended, to be. Without those struggles, we would have no reason to reach higher—to grow in our spirits, minds, and even our bodies—and to learn how to fly to greater heights than we ever imagined we could when we started this beautiful but tough journey.

That is just the beginning of the value of troubles with our toiling. In no other single activity or part of our lives do we become more closely tied to God and his purpose for us than in our work. Most of us spend more of our time at work than we do anywhere else. The trials and tribulations that we encounter in our occupations give us the opportunity to see what God intends for us, to learn how to live lives focused on loving and support-ing ourselves and others simultaneously, to learn how to love our neighbors as ourselves. The habits and lifestyle that we develop through work, and the problems associated with it, will be more responsible for our innermost development, personality, and ulti-mate behavior patterns than just about any other single part of our lives.

This does not happen overnight. Sometimes it takes years of struggle before we learn how to simultaneously support ourselves and love others at the same time, while we realize our ability and the importance of doing so.

The lessons and examples are there all around us: from the Bible to famous and not-so-famous tales of those who learned how to prosper by the sweat of their brow in a way that simulta-neously helped the world. Usually these people had to suffer along the way before they could see the light. Maybe that is just God's way of forcing all that fluid out of our egos and into our hearts so that we can beat for others while also taking care of ourselves. If we could be successful, make a good living, and live in a world that was utopia—without having to work—would any of us care to struggle for others?

Even God Has to Work!

God actually provides the perfect example for us to follow at work and a wonderful view of that work. God "worked" for six days to create the world, resting only on the seventh. He did so to create a world not for himself but for us, so that we might have dominion over it and so that we may enjoy it. He then created us in his image and commanded us to do his will. Remember, too, that God takes pleasure in his work, pronouncing at the end of each day that what he created was "good," and that it brought new life. As he saw fit, God kept enhancing and adding to that life, to create a joyous and full world.

His example is the greatest one we could possibly emulate in our own work, to create something beautiful and great for others. Through such great contribution we will be rewarded with what we need to sustain ourselves in many ways—physically, spiritually, and emotionally—as well in terms of the love and respect we receive from others and society for our needed contributions. This is the greatest goal we can have.

All of these characteristics of work are something to strive for within our own labor. Whether we have or don't have these facets to our work, either way it is a source of inspiration, to revel in the good we are doing and the satisfaction it is providing, or to wake up to adapt our perspective or change our occupations.

There are some occupations that may not be healthy in general or just not right for us because they do not allow us to utilize our God-given talents and desires in a way that benefits others. Then our dissatisfaction or struggle within these occupations truly calls us to take our labor elsewhere. But we should truly evaluate the source of unhappiness before deciding we must change our jobs.

It is a challenge to see things when we are surrounded by a "me-focused" culture that tells us that success for the sake of fame, wealth, and self is all that is important. In that culture, it is easy to lose sight of our work's purpose, work's pleasure, and our own calling. In that environment, it is difficult to see the value of hard work itself, let alone the possible value of tragedy and tribulation connected to that hard work to lead us to better places and better perspectives. That world is simply one in which the only questions we ask are "What do I have?" and "What don't I have?"

Too Good to Work for You

Ashley Simpson is a big recording star. At the age of twenty-one, after only two albums, she has already sold enough and accrued enough success to call her own shots. Millions of people have spent around $15 of their hard-earned money to hear Ashley do her thing on a CD. That means that a whole lot of people were willing to contribute to Ashley's being able to do what she loves and make a whole lot of money doing it, which is fair because she is entertaining them. They believe she is adding something good and pleasurable to their lives, and in exchange they are willing to add to her pleasurable and secure lifestyle.

Sounds like that would be enough to convince Ms. Simpson to continue to do all that she could, within reason, to satisfy her fans, so that she could continue to earn and to deserve their purchases. On the contrary, she says that she no longer needs to concern herself with what the buying public may want or what would be entertaining to those she profits by. She believes that her "art" is only for her amusement.

"I love to sing. It's a joy to me. I don't do it for anyone else—I do it for me," declared Simpson after the release of her second album. Simpson continued in her self-absorbed diatribe that has become all-too-familiar a line spoken by celebrities: *"I've had to learn that my voice is the most important one."*[1]

What is most significant about Simpson's remarks is the sentiment and reasoning behind them. Simpson probably did not intend for them to sound selfish. On the contrary, she is most likely another victim of an ultramodern philosophy that says what you do for a living has nothing to do with any duty to society or helping others. Instead it is all about what *you* want and what makes *you* happy without any real regard for what society needs or wants.

This philosophy was expressed most notably in the second half of the twentieth century, and it is diametrically different than what existed in the first half of the century. In the earlier period, America's "greatest generation," as Tom Brokaw coined it, fought a war and built a thriving economy on the principles of hard work, dedication, and chipping in. They found great gratification from fulfilling responsibilities to their friends, family, and society, while making the best living they could. Even as late as the early sixties, President John F. Kennedy was able to inspire a nation with the call to "Think not what your country can do for you, but what you can do for your country."

However, a very different mentality took its first hold in America with the arts of the pensive poets and novelists that were part of the Beat Generation. Led by the likes of Jack Kerouac, his classic manifesto *On the Road* is practically a how-to guide on dropping out of mainstream America in order to travel down the road of self-satiation of basic whims and desires. Though it disguised itself as a rejection of consumerism and the rat race, it was really an even worse form of greed, not for money or economic prosperity, but for basic and guttural self-satisfaction.

This philosophy trickled down to the rest of the arts through actors and musicians in the sixties, expressing their craft in terms of what they felt—method acting. Soon that expression of personal desires became not only the means through which they practiced their art, but it also became the whole purpose of their art—to get things, to get the lifestyle they wanted. The term *finding yourself* replaced the historically popular *finding your way*. Finding your purpose and calling in the world was transmogrified into simply finding whatever you desired.

What makes it so flawed is that, while we can never detach ourselves completely from the needs and demands of others, we can still be rewarded by others so we can live the lives we want. In truth, we work to make a living not because it is something that sounds fun and self-gratifying. We do so because we *need* to make a living. The genius of God's design is that we cannot survive on our own. We need help, and we get that help by giving that help in the form of our labor. We are then rewarded by those *we* help with *their* help, usually in the form of money at the most basic level. The principle of providing a needed service applies to anything that you want to do for a living.

Learning to Love Her Job

Mindy was a teacher who never really wanted to be a teacher but always desired to be a writer. She never gave up on that dream, and as she was pushing sixty, she was published for the first time, writing about kids for a national women's magazine. She was ecstatic and was actually even happy that she had never realized her dream when she was younger. *"It made me search for meaning in my life, and I found it helping others as a teacher,"* explained Mindy. *"If I had achieved my dream of being a writer right away, then that would never have happened. I also never would have felt all the joy that I have experienced over the last twenty years with these kids. And now I have a whole lot to write about too."*

Mindy came from the feel-good generation that first promoted doing whatever you wanted to do. When she became pregnant in her last year of college and the father of the child fled, all changed very quickly. When she graduated, she immediately needed to make a living. While a career in writing was risky, teaching was available and paid the bills. *"I wanted desperately to be a writer,"* she explains. *"I grew up reading. Gertrude Stein was my hero. But I figured I could teach for a few years until I became a best-selling novelist."*

Mindy never wrote the great American novel, or at least not yet, but along the way she realized something that she never thought she would. She was living the great American dream, making a living and a life while contributing to her community and her world.

Just a few years after getting her first job as a third-grade teacher at the same school she had attended as a kid, she was awarded teacher of the year. Amazingly, Mindy still was not crazy about teaching, yet it was a stable job that put food on the table for her and her healthy and hungry little boy, Brett. *"Every time I would get frustrated at work, I just thought about him,"* recalls Mindy. *"He was the reason I was doing it. And that really started to change the way I looked at the job in general when he grew to be the same age as the children I was teaching."*

After three decades of teaching, she never wants to quit, even if she hits it big as a writer. *"So much of what I know, of what I think and feel, I got from this job,"* said Mindy. *"This is what I was meant to do. The writing is just a way of sharing it with others."*

We All Have to Eat!

Mindy's story certainly provides "food for thought" anytime you get down about your job. This does not mean you cannot look for a career that you enjoy or that you should not leave a job that you hate in order to find your calling. Perhaps first take a look at what we have and the reasons we do not want it, as well as the reasons why we want something else.

John van Hengle was nursing a divorce at the same time that he walked away from a public-relations career because he was just not happy. It was the sixties, and he wandered like so many others did during that generation, trying to find out what to do with his life.

With no job and no real direction, he took a job driving a bus for St. Mary's Church in Phoenix that led him to helping out in the church dining room that fed the hungry. One day he mentioned to one of the priests that they needed a warehouse or "clearing house" as he put it for all the extra food that grocery stores and restaurants threw away each year. The priest told van Hengle that he would get him a location and some funding if he would run it. Van Hengle agreed and within a year, St. Mary's Food Bank, the world's first food bank for the hungry, was born. As the story goes, a few days later, as van Hengle was wondering where they would get seed money to start the ball rolling, a man who heard about his idea strolled in and handed van Hengle a check for $10,000.

Over the next several decades, St. Mary's Food Bank became a major force in social-justice programs to feed the hungry. It distributed about 250,000 pounds of food in its first year, and in 2005, about 60 million pounds. Today thousands of similar food banks exist all over the world.

For that, we can all thank van Hengle and his job troubles, which led him to his calling. When van Hengle wanted a job or a career in which he felt fulfilled and discovered that it was not public relations, he did not get bogged down in the tragedy, nor did he isolate himself from the world in his despair. He did just the opposite, reached out and looked for a realistic way to be a part of it. He had the faith and the perseverance to hang on through the struggle.

Incidentally, van Hengle's journey led me to write my first editorial article about child poverty when, as a young reporter, I interviewed the media director of St. Mary's Food Bank. This planted the seeds of practical social justice in my heart that blossomed years later. Thus the positive effect of one man's job problems just keep multiplying.

Not knowing what to do with your life is a common problem. Finding yourself is fine, if within the context of the greater needs of the world. None of us is an island, no matter how much we may want to believe we are. We cannot just go off and live in the woods by ourselves, fending only for ourselves.

One person who tried to do that but still found the answers to his occupational questions in the hearts of others was Yvon Chouinard, the founder and owner of the outdoor-clothing company Patagonia. A French Canadian immigrant who moved with his family to California in the 1940s, Chouinard grew up feeling isolated because he spoke little English. He took solace learning how to hunt and fish, spending most of his time alone in the wilderness. He soon found a passion for rock climbing, and after finishing high school lived off the land while he enjoyed his passion. He still had no idea what he wanted to do for a living, and he was not financially secure. The only thing he knew was that he loved climbing, and he yearned for the outdoors, so he went and literally lived in them. He became a blacksmith and began making his own climbing supplies. Living off wild game and sometimes resorting to eating cat food, he realized he needed to make money as well. Whenever he climbed, he ran into nice people who always needed climbing supplies, like the ones he made. So he started selling some of his designs to make ends meet and to give his new friends products that would help and protect them at the same time. Since he was making these products for those he met and befriended along the way, it was most important that the products be of the highest quality and safety.

Soon he was supporting himself by selling equipment from the back of his car and by the 1970s, his company was the largest domestic supplier of climbing equipment in the United States. He diversified and began offering clothing and accessories for everything outdoors. Chouinard presently claims to ignore the bottom line, concerning himself rather with ethical management strategies, such as producing high-quality products regardless of the cost; providing employees with on-site child care and flextime; using environmentally responsive production methods; and controlling growth to about 5 percent a year, while giving away 1 percent toward environmental causes. Still the company is performing by leaps and bounds, selling about $2.5 million a year. That's a lot of growth and a great deal of socially responsive behavior for a company started by a guy who just wanted to climb rocks by himself.[2]

Fired—UP!

What about getting fired? Can there be anything worse than finding your calling, the thing you love and want to do for a living more than anything else in the world, and having it ripped away from you, beyond your control?

Walt Disney was fired from his first drawing job at an ad agency because they felt he was not a very good artist. It was understandable that the future father of animation exhibited less-than-stellar talents at the job since it busied him drawing rough sketches of farm equipment for which he was neither excited nor inspired. He humbled himself to go back to his old job temporarily working at the post office while he started freelance drawing. *Now* he was inspired and motivated by the fact that somebody actually had hired him to draw for a living. In his mind, the fact he had the skill to convince someone to pay him for his drawing was all the evidence he needed that he *could* do this for a living. Of course, we all know what happened after that. He started his own company and came up with a character, Mickey Mouse, that brought joy to millions around the world, simultaneously bringing him a great deal of joy and prosperity.

Steve Jobs, the legendary visionary and creator of Apple Computers and the iPod, also got fired at the height of his career and from his own company. After starting with nothing at the age of twenty and building Apple Computers with blood, sweat, and ideas from the ground up, he put his trust in a brilliant executive he wooed away from Coke, someone he believed he could trust with running the company coincident with his vision. Instead, the executive convinced the entire board of directors to take the company in another direction and to dismiss the man who started it all.

At thirty, Jobs had lost the entire focus and love of his life, and he was devastated. He considered leaving the industry he loved completely and running away from it all. Then it occurred to him that getting fired from Apple was perhaps the best thing that could have happened to him. He went through a very extensive process of self-evaluation. During the next five years, he thought about ideas that could help others and give the world something it very much needed. He started a company called *NeXT* that did marginally well and another named *Pixar Animation Studios* that became quite successful. *Pixar* became the leader in computer-animated feature films, creating the first one ever, *Toy Story,* then followed with blockbuster successes like *Finding Nemo, A Bug's Life,* and *The Incredibles.*

With a new attitude toward what he did for a living, he also changed the way he lived his personal life. He opened his heart to meeting the love of his life, got married, and started a family.

While Jobs was going through his transition, Apple was going through its own evolution. With Jobs gone and Apple lagging badly profit-wise, the man who fired him was let go. Then, after a couple of other failed CEOs, the company's new leader brought Jobs back into the fold when he bought Jobs's company *NeXT* to use its operating system for the next generation of *Apples.* Within a year or so, Jobs was back running his company, taking Apple back to the top with his groundbreaking ideas, plus a little maturity.[3]

Sometimes the tragedy of being fired is far better than the tragedy that might have been had we not been fired. In other words, maybe getting fired teaches us something and changes us in a way that we need to be changed. Without that experience we might have languished forever in a less-than-desirable state.

This was the case with Michael Finkel.[4] He spent decades working his way up the ladder as a journalist until finally his dream came true: he landed a job at the *New York Times Magazine,* a job that most journalists would have given their right arm for and so the pressure to perform was intense.

Finkel was sent to West Africa to write a story about slavery allegations about the chocolate trade. The story was a tough one. He was in the middle of nowhere, chasing down a dangerous story involving heavy-hitting smugglers of human cargo. He needed someone who knew about the whole ugly mess, not only to tell him about it, but also to go public about it, knowing they could be killed for doing so. Also, there was a language barrier.

Meanwhile, back in New York, his editors were undoubtedly hounding him for his story. So Finkel did what many a reporter would be ashamed to admit they have done when pressed into such a corner. He took all the information he had found and threw it into the mouth of an imaginary character, one that was too good to be true. He made up a source, and he lied to his editors about it.

Like most lies, it did not have a lot of staying power. When editors realized that too much about his incredible story was not checking out, he got fired. This resulted in self-regret as he questioned his identity now that he had lost all that he ever wanted and that which he identified himself with. Ironically he found out that his actual identity *had* been stolen, quite literally, at the same time. A call from FBI agents informed him that a murderer on their "Ten Most-Wanted" list had adopted his identity.

Christian Longo had murdered his wife and three children in Oregon, then fled to Mexico. He had been impersonating Finkel—just another duplicitous act in a lifetime of lies and deceptions. A lying murderer pretending to be someone else by stealing Finkel's identity at the same time he himself was reflecting on getting fired for his deceit was too coincidental to fathom, let alone resist.

With no job and no future unless he found a story to redeem his character and put himself back on top, Finkel decided to meet the murderer who had lied his way into his life, hoping for a story, this time a real one to tell. So he wrote a book about Longo, about his life of lies and Finkel's own lies—the ones that led him to telling this story. Along the way Finkel saw what lies can do, the isolation and the damage that they can lead to at their worst, and he saw through this murderer's eyes his own deadly flaws. Through an incredible coincidence, a murderer's dark duplicity showed him his. Oddly enough, it all happened thanks to his getting fired. Only through his fall did he rise to become an esteemed author and, more important, a man of integrity.

Throwing It Away?

Finkel's story hit home for me especially since it recalls my own transformation. I became a writer because I loved to write, and I wanted to make the world a better place. Also I wanted fame and fortune as most young men do after growing up in a culture where I saw it held up as the goal. I was ambitious, and after splitting from a small-time job in Arizona, I headed for Los Angeles. In just two weeks, I was chasing down celebrities for the *National Enquirer*. I rose up the ranks and then went to work for *People* magazine and then back to the tabloids as a senior editor. I interviewed everyone from the famous to the felonious. However, I was miserable and did not know the reasons.

It all came crashing down when the Columbine story hit. The world of journalism had reached its lowest point with the insensitive and sensational coverage nationwide, making it appear as if every child in America was in danger of being shot at their desks, even as the rate of violence in schools was decreasing year after year. A little voice inside me told me—no more! I went home that day on leave and quit a month later, respectfully explaining my conflict of conscience to my boss.

Not knowing what to do, I reached down deep and tried to figure out something. I had pitched a series of book ideas recently. One of them garnered the interest of a publisher, a collection of stories of people who had overcome adversity through the power of love. Writing this book would be good for my soul, I figured, and somebody wanted to buy it. What I would do after that, I had no idea. Within a year, I had written and published my first book, then a sequel, a third, and so on. Suddenly I knew what I wanted and was meant to do. Now I share inspiring stories, thoughts, and anecdotes with readers all over the world, and I get more satisfaction than I ever could have dreamed.

The answers, the light, and the relief from our struggle do not always come quickly. Sometimes it takes years, and we may spend many of those years ignoring the positive potential of our struggles, only to wake up one day to see the light. Sometimes we see what we want only after we give up or lose all that we had, such as was the case in my own life.

Consider the story of Tim Buso.[5] From the time he was a boy all he ever wanted to do was to be around planes. After getting out of the military, he landed a job as an air-traffic controller with the FAA and was ecstatic. In August 1981, the thirty-year-old controller made the decision to join 12,000 of his fellow controllers to strike for better pay and working conditions. When President Reagan ordered them to return to their jobs or be fired, he didn't. He was fired along with about 11,500 controllers.

Over the next two decades his life went from bad to worse. With no other real skills or training, and with the scorn of many of those within his community who felt that he had compromised the public's safety for selfish reasons, Buso struggled to get by on low-paying odd jobs, drifting from one failure to another. Even a management position at McDonald's didn't work out. As the money dwindled, so did his marriage, finally ending in divorce.

He did whatever honest work he could find to pay the bills. Then one day while working at a part-time painting job for $5 an hour to pay the rent, his life came full circle. A union painter picketed the gas station that had hired Buso since he was not in the painters' union, threatening to take away the little work he could find. After explaining that he was a union man as well and that the picketing threatened the only work he could find, the picketing stopped. The irony of the situation was all too clear.

Buso dealt with the pain, the struggle, and the unhappiness by turning to alcohol. He scraped by on $10,000 or less a year until 1984 when he landed a well-paying job as a postal worker. It was not the love of his life but it paid the bills and helped him to get his life back on track.

Things were not all bad, in fact, quite to the contrary. He stopped drinking. At the post office he met his second wife and fell in love. Then President Clinton lifted the ban on hiring back the fired controllers, and he got the courage to file another application with the FAA. In 1998 he got a call from the FAA asking him if he was interested in being an air-traffic controller again. A month later he was back on the job with a new life.

As a young man he was on top of the world with the job of his dreams. Then for years he chastised himself for going on strike. Twenty years of adversity made him realize it was not about him and what he could get out of his job, but about what he could give. The opportunity to do something he loved and was good at while contributing to society was amazing. Going through his own "recession" is what it took to wake him up to a better view of work and a better view of the purpose and potential of work.

Earning Your Soul

Though all these people rebounded from their job troubles and attained success, they had one other thing in common too, that their career troubles led them all to greater understanding of work and the problems and opportunities it brought. Yet they still all pursued careers that they had an interest in, and they learned to look at work as more of a chance to serve than simply to achieve their own personal desires. This attitude inspires a greater purpose that makes you want to help out more, it drives you, and it gives you the support of the others that you are helping to do the same thing out there in the world.

Sometimes that might make you even leave a job in which you were very successful. Nobel Peace Prize recipient Albert Schweitzer walked away from a profitable career as a professor and a world-renowned writer and musician. Why? When he was twenty-eight, he read a report on the dire health conditions in Africa, and he decided that the best way for him to devote himself "to the direct service of humanity" would be as a doctor. After six years of medical school, he went to Africa and started a hospital in an old chicken house, the only building he could find available. In the next nine months, he treated over two thousand people!

Or like Buso's case, sometimes we figure out our calling to serve only after we have had the opportunity to do it taken away from us. There are a million ways we can all react to the problems that befall us in our careers. When we choose to respond in ways that are helpful to the community of mankind rather than simply reacting to our own emotions, we usually wind up reaping the benefit.

The daughter of poor immigrant farmers, Louise Raggio was a smart and ambitious young woman who went to law school at night for five years while she struggled to raise three sons. She loved the law and wanted to help those who were deprived of its protections. However, in 1952 in Dallas, she didn't get very far when she graduated and discovered that law firms didn't hire women except as secretaries. Her inability to get a job led her to start her own firm out of her kitchen, writing wills for $15 a piece. When she wanted to expand her efforts and start a real full-fledged firm, she learned that women in Texas, like many other states, had almost no property rights. That made it impossible for them to get a loan, sign a bail bond, or undertake most of the steps necessary to own a business, without the written support of a husband. Infuriated and frustrated by this personal career obstacle, she set out to change the law for all women. It took her decades fighting the good fight, but she eventually won. Her efforts achieved the 1967 passage of the Marital Property Act, which gave women limited control over some of the property a woman earned in marriage. She has been recognized for laying the groundwork for the Equal Credit Opportunity Act, which made it illegal for lenders to discriminate on the basis of race, color, religion, national origin, age, or marital status.

Raggio went on to successfully sue many corporations for sex discrimination, allowing women entry into a slew of different professions. She practiced law well into her eighties and was the first woman elected director of the State Bar of Texas. All because she could not do the job she wanted to do.[6]

Back in the 1980s, Howard Rubin lost $350 million trading securities for Merrill Lynch. He spent most of his life compensating for an amazingly powerful fear of failure. One could imagine after his cataclysmic demise, those feelings would have been magnified tenfold. He came out of it not only with an amazing ability to handle failure, but he also was hired by another trader to ferret out reckless and irresponsible behavior because he understood it so well. Again all because he could not do the job he wanted to do.[7]

Minna Vallentine gave her heart and soul to a software firm, only to get laid off in her late fifties when they downsized. She could not find a job that paid anywhere near what she had been making before, so she adjusted her life. Then she asked herself what she would do *if money were no object*. The answer was simple: teach people to read. She began a business called the *Reading Doctor* and to pay the bills while she got her business started, she taught immigrants to read through a partnership with the local school systems. She went from six figures to barely surviving financially, but the satisfaction that she found more than compensated for it. She learned how to live more simply, to want and need less, to shop less, to not eat out, and to relearn how to enjoy simple free activities like a walk in the park or a bicycle ride.[8]

You probably never heard of technocrat millionaire Kamran Elahian. He changed the world because he got fired. On April Fool's Day in 1992, the thirty-eight-year-old was dismissed from Moments, the company he had started after making a name for himself as the cofounder of the multi-billion-dollar *Cirrus Logic, Inc.* As chairman, president, and CEO of Moments, he was a dynamo of innovation when he created a computer that could recognize a user's handwriting. He made the cover of twenty magazines for it. The only problem was that, back in the early

1990s, this great technological miracle was not yet economically viable. In other words, it did not sell, and he got fired. When the company itself went bankrupt six months later, he was emotionally destroyed.

Coming from Iran on his own when he was eighteen to start a new life, he had worked his way through school into a high-paying engineering job at Hewlett Packard. Then he had the courage to leave which eventually led to success at Cirrus. He had gained recognition and lost it.

He went "underground" for a year, just thinking about where he had come from, where he would go, and what he would do. Reflecting on his youth, he was struck that what we had in this country he saw none of in Iran when he was growing up. He was not thinking of money and materialism but the opportunities that came from the availability of education and information. He reasoned that many of the world's problems stemmed from that isolation. He immediately sat down and committed himself to a mission statement for his life—to find a way to give people in remote areas of the world the ability to connect to the rest of it.

Over the next six years he started telecommunications companies that "introduced the world to the third world," by bringing the Internet to 5,800 schools in twenty-five countries, and setting up Internet learning camps in distant and remote places like Burundi. He was back on top, and the world was better for it.[9]

L-*earning* a Living!

Each one of the people in this chapter took different specific paths to dealing with their job troubles. Each of us should also realize we are all capable of contributing through our work to the world around us, no matter how long it might take for us to figure out how. Whether you get fired, you quit, you cannot find a job, or you just hate your job, focusing on innately worthwhile reasons for doing that job or for finding another are more likely to get you where you want to be than focusing on where you were. That led all these people to a reality check, acknowledging what had happened and why, while also realizing the potential ahead of them. They focused on people in their lives that needed them, people that loved them and supported them, and people in general. Then they thought how they could love others and help people, including themselves, with their skills, their ideas, and their efforts. That made them realize how important they were, which led them to greater feelings of self-esteem and appreciation, not arrogance. They were valuable because of how they could serve the world in their occupations or positions.

5

Shine On!

Divorce, Bad Breakups, and Loneliness

Breaking up hurts—really hurts. Whether it is the sadness that comes at the end of a long-term relationship or the horrible life-altering destruction that occurs when a divorce tears lives and families apart, hearts are broken into two. Despair, loneliness, and depression leave most people asking, Why bother to consider love at all? It is also then that we must look beyond the blame and pain and into our very integral need to grow, to respect ourselves, and to regard others as God intends us to—within a mutually respectful relationship. We must think about all the goodness, joy, and grace that come to us in relationships, even the one that did not work out in the end.

Failed relationships can also inspire us to ask whether *this* relationship was taking us in the wrong direction, or was self-abusive or codependent. If so, is our desire to keep it going really what God wants for us? Perhaps the answer to our confusion and our pain will lie beyond the tragedy of the breakup itself and within the development of our ability to make it through such events with dignity and love in our hearts and a commitment to mutually respectful relationships in the future. Through the breakup and the turmoil we can find the strength, the inner mettle, and the growth we need to make our lives and our love work better.

Therein lies one of the most important yet misunderstood ideas behind relationships. While we are looking for what we want in a mate, we discover what we want and need in *us,* and in doing so we discover who we are, who we want to be, and, in many cases, who we wish we were not. By trying to love another selflessly, we are forced for a moment to see the world through their eyes, and that gives us the rare opportunity to see ourselves honestly.

The pain of a breakup can shake you to the core of your being. That is exactly where you need to get in order to grow— at the core of your being. Pain in that most central part of your being motivates you to do something about it, and though there are some dangerous and negative ways to deal with that pain, there are also a whole lot of positive ways.

Relationship problems are some of the most emotionally and mentally jarring experiences that exist outside of dealing with the death of a loved one. No matter what anybody says, you will hurt. Anybody who tells you differently is far more out of their mind than you are when you are in the midst of one of these minideaths.

But ask yourself this question: When it comes to your worst relationship or the hardest breakup, would you rather the relationship had never happened? Would you erase the time and experience? Unless the relationship was marred by some kind of extreme abuse, most people would say no. Because after the pain, or at least most of it, is gone, what remains is the knowledge, the memories, and the love that you experienced and you learned how to give. All things considered, loving someone is a pretty great thing, an opportunity that we should never regret having had, and one that we should never be afraid to have again.

It's Over. But What About the Love You Didn't Lose?

So you just lost the love of your life, either because of something you did, they did, both, or circumstances beyond your control. The first step is to stop reacting desperately to the loss of love. Don't panic! The same rules apply to this tragedy as all the others. Don't lose control. If you do, then all that will come of this will be more pain, suffering, and tragedy because you will make bad decisions that will neither enable you to regain your ability to love or to find new love. Avoid the temptation to fall into despair. You need to believe that this is not the end of the world. *What* you have and *who* you have ready to help you are a good place to start.

That is not to say that you do not feel a tremendous loss and the pain that accompanies that loss. Of course you do, and you do not need to deny or conceal that pain. The positive potential lies deep within the acceptance of that pain and suffering. That does not mean you should let this tragedy lead to many others that might occur by abusing yourself or those around you.

Keep reminding yourself that a mate is not the whole point of your life. God did not create us solely to mate; he also intended us to love him and each other outside of the romance of marriage and relationships. The same opportunities abound for someone alone because of a breakup that exist for those who haven't yet met their mate. There is a world of people waiting to be loved and who want to love you, not only in a romantic way. Allowing yourself to be blessed by those that you love and who honestly love you is not only paramount to your growth—it is survival!

Learn how to love those people while you are temporarily restrained from loving a mate. Love is love in the end, and it is all connected. The greatest and most obvious source of that love after a breakup is the fountain of friends and family around you ready and willing to help you through.

A breakup is going to make you question everything about your life, your identity, and your beliefs. That type of mental and emotional surgery hurts, as do the feelings of worry and concern, even anger, about the individual we have lost.

People date in various ways. Some date just to get something from another person, whether it is money, sex, or attention. Some date to take a chance by exposing themselves to another individual and taking the risk. Dating is also an opportunity to cherish the love that you have received from the other person and to pass it around. Think about it: If a mate is God's gift, then it would make sense that God could speak to our hearts through that individual in a way that nobody else can, teaching us how to love.

For all of our relationships, what is most important is not whether they work out but what they allow us to become. In relationships we see the *potential* to love another individual and to be loved totally and unconditionally, whether you actually accomplish this. If you were not treated as such, or you did not treat another individual with this respect, you are probably going to be overcome with feelings of regret, anger, confusion, or all of these. That is not only frustration over the relationship ending, but also a feeling of loss of the divine possibilities that existed within the romance that were never realized or that were removed once they were. That can inspire you, spur you, to seek a different type of mate, one who is willing to return your honest love or to augment your behavior to better deserve one who already does.

The Value of You

Breakups make you grow even when you don't necessarily want to. They force you to consider who you are, who you want to be, how you behave, how you live. They can make you feel like your whole life is flashing in front of your eyes as if you are about to die. Their conclusions are a form of death. However, breakups are also a form of rebirth and resurrection. In many cases they may even be what brings about the rebirth and resurrection of the actual relationships that we believe we have lost.

You could spend your life going from one relationship to another, never even thinking about who you are, how you date, what you want in an individual, what you want in your life, or the way you treat others. On the other hand, remember that when you are shaken to the core of your being, you now have the opportunity to evaluate that core of your being. The key is using the time and the pain constructively to learn and grow, so that you and your relationships have a chance to recover and grow too.

The End—FOR REAL

Wanting not to break up and working hard to prevent it do not mean you will succeed. Despite all our best efforts, sometimes the walls fall down around your heart. When they do, it feels like the end of your world, like there is no tomorrow or at least not the one you counted on, thrusting you into what seems like a cloud of meaningless mayhem. But you *can* find the meaning in the pain, the confusion, and the emotional turmoil to inspire you to examine the why and how in your life and in life in general.

Even though a relationship did not work, it does not mean that *we* do not work. Think of it as an opportunity to search our souls and our minds for an understanding of what happened, what we want, why we want it, and where we want to go from here. As long as we do not get mired in the tragedy or try to pretend it did not happen, that is exactly what breakups inspire us to do. Maybe we are choosing people that do not fit, or we are unable to commit to those that do, or we are still learning how to better determine who we should entrust our hearts to. Maybe it was just not the right time. Ultimately, all these things are good to find out. Remember, the wisdom in a breakup does not lie in us hating ourselves for what happened but in the understanding and the growth it brings. Sometimes that means accepting that someone else does not love us anymore or possibly never did, while still realizing we are worthy of being loved in spite of that.

Suzanne was a twenty-four-year-old single, printing rep in Iowa when she met her future husband, who was thirty years old and divorced. They were married just three months after their first date and quickly had two children. Suzanne became a stay-at-home mom, and her husband went away on business trips. Ten years later with her husband traveling all the time leaving her at home with the kids, she was frustrated. She got her master's degree and her PhD. She became involved with politics, first working for the Equal Rights Initiative in Iowa, eventually going to work for a state legislator. She even won an award for her efforts, the Christine Wilson Medal for Equality and Justice. Although her husband did not object to any of it, he really didn't care much about it either. Suzanne said, *"When I won the award, he said [to me], 'I had no idea that you did anything worth getting an award for.' I probably would have run for office if I wasn't married to him. But I knew he couldn't handle that, and then the marriage wouldn't have worked. I grew up with the belief that you do whatever you have to do to protect your marriage."*

"There's happy and there's silent," said Suzanne. *"I loved him, and I thoroughly delighted in his sense of humor. There were red flags going up all over the place. But I didn't want to acknowledge them."*

That was until she had to. One day in 1990, after three horrible years dealing with his mother's illness, he simply left without out a word of explanation. *"I thought he was coming home to show me his new BMW; he was there to tell me that he just couldn't stand our marriage anymore,"* recalled Suzanne. *"He wanted to be happy, and so he was leaving. I didn't know that you could physically hurt that much from a breakup until then, and I didn't know what to do to make it stop hurting."*

She had never been that involved in her faith, although she was baptized and confirmed, and sang in the church choir. When a friend suggested she go to see her pastor for some counseling, it opened her eyes to a deeper relationship with God. *"That he would provide for me in times like these never occurred to me before,"* said Suzanne. *"The idea that God doesn't abandon us, I never thought of that. The Lord might have been my shepherd, but I wasn't a sheep was my attitude."*

Meanwhile, her husband returned the next month as if nothing had ever happened. *"He said he was sorry, and he moved back in and that was the end of it,"* explained Suzanne. *"When the kids asked what happened, he told them that he was back, and nothing had changed and that was that."*

Since Suzanne had already started down a road to deepening her faith and her understanding of herself, she figured why not continue. Soon afterward, her brother admitted he was an alcoholic and Suzanne's newfound faith helped her to comfort him. She filled her shelves with books on spirituality and healing and would spend hours talking about them with her brother.

While she was growing deeper spiritually, her husband was not honest even with the therapist they went to see about why he left in the first place. He treated any attempt to find out what he was feeling when he left her as an attack, one from which Suzanne always retreated. *"So we moved on as if it never happened,"* said Suzanne. *"His limit was the limit on our intimacy. And that included sexual, emotional, and spiritual."*

Then in 1995, her husband learned three days before Christmas he had what doctors believed was terminal cancer of the esophagus. They faced the illness together, and Suzanne's awakened spirituality inspired both of them. Surgery to remove the cancerous tumors was successful and amazingly within a year, doctors told them the disease was gone. The miracle affirmed Suzanne's faith and commitment to God.

However, John was not equally inspired. He decided to retire after that, and he quickly grew bored. While she was joyously delving into her spirituality, he wanted nothing to do with it or with her work, which was picking up as his wound down. *"I was active in my church, and I had a full life,"* explained Suzanne. *"But John was miserable. It seemed like he just wanted to be unhappy."*

After attending his high-school reunion, he found some joy in helping a former classmate who was diagnosed with cancer. Unfortunately he was also inspired by the former homecoming queen with whom he began an affair that night. A year later, just a few weeks before Christmas, after thirty years of marriage, her husband walked in the door, sat down, and told her he wanted a divorce, and he did not want to talk about it. *"I watched the clock as he spoke to me because I was in shock,"* recalled Suzanne, *"It was all of two minutes from start to finish. It was over just like that."*

Suzanne moved into a winter condo they had in Arizona, and there she began to rebuild her life. She was miserable and confused, and wanted her husband back. Yet to her amazement, for the first time in a long time she began enjoying life. *"My son and daughter came to stay one weekend, and we just had fun,"* said Suzanne. *"We went shopping for new clothes, cooked, hung out, and didn't clean up all weekend. My husband used to be so controlling and so anal that he never would allow any of that."*

She began counseling through the Catholic Retreat Center and there she realized the problems that her marriage had and the issues she needed to confront about herself that she had been avoiding. *"I didn't want my marriage to end, but I realized I also didn't want my old life back either,"* explained Suzanne. *"For years he refused to offer any intimacy in the relationship, so what did I really lose? There was nothing to get back. I was just used to it. My heart was broken open, but then I saw all the gifts that lay inside."*

After finally conceding the marriage was over, she thrust herself even deeper into her faith, her family, and the work she loved. She got to know her children better than ever. She sold her vacation home for a good profit and bought a new house of her own just a few blocks from her daughter in northern California, a place she always wanted to live but which her husband hated. She reacquainted herself with old friends she had not seen in years, people her husband was not very fond of. She resumed work on her writing, finishing up a collection of stories of influential women in politics. She lost weight and got into better physical shape. The ordeal opened up a whole new relationship with her mother who now spoke openly with her about the pain of enduring her father's infidelity.

Since the breakup, she and her husband have spoken less than five minutes in person, communicating almost entirely by e-mail, which does not surprise Suzanne. *"He still doesn't know me at all,"* said Suzanne. *"And that's how it would have continued for the rest of our lives, I'm sure of it. But now at least I know me."*

Suzanne's case is extreme. Despite the shocking suddenness of her husband's two departures and the trauma that followed, she finally got her wish after all. She was awakened to all the love she did have inside of her by the stark realization of her husband's lack of it.

Life After Love

The opportunity to realize we can and should be vessels of God's love within a relationship can also inspire us to realize selfless wisdom and love for and from others outside of that relationship. Once we get over the initial shock and pain, that should spur us on to go and love some more. We may find another blessed mate. We may even wind up back with the one we loved, only this time for all the right reasons and with the right attitude. Or we may be directed to experience love in a way we never even imagined. We must push ourselves into the company of those we love and those who love us, sometimes kicking and screaming, so that we can receive the wisdom that God sends to us there.

A breakup can be God's little wake-up call of self-discovery, letting us know we are being called to a mission, something beyond the relationship and even beyond ourselves, a higher calling if you will, like the case of Mother Antonia.[1]

Born Mary Clark, the blonde beauty with the glamour-girl good looks grew up in the 1920s, living the life of luxury in the California sunshine of Beverly Hills. She was even offered a job as a dancer by the famous director/choreographer Busby Berkeley. Growing up near Hollywood made her immune to fame's allure.

She wanted something more meaningful, to be a wife and a mother, she thought. She did not need a rich man, just a simple hard-working real man.

At twenty, she thought she met that man and married him. Even though she loved him with all her heart, he could never hold down a job, and his fear of commitment and his gambling habit were ruining the marriage as well. After tragically losing her first child, she grew deeper in her Catholic faith, while he grew more addicted to gambling. He spent less and less time at home, and she grew less enchanted with the marriage.

They persevered to have two children, a boy and a girl. He gambled more and more, and she felt more and more distant from him. When Mary finally left him, she was only twenty-four years old, had two children, and was facing the worst shame a woman could bring upon herself at the time—divorce. She moved into a little apartment, got two jobs to get by, and lamented her situation.

Alone and afraid, she ran into the arms of a stable, wealthy man who could take care of her, and she married him outside the Church, meaning she could no longer receive communion. He protected and loved her family, and she respected him for that. She had five more children with him, but their personalities never clicked. She wanted a partner and a friend. He wanted a traditional stay-at-home wife. She wanted to make a difference. He wanted to make a fortune.

Now provided with all of her worldly concerns, she began reflecting more deeply into herself and into what God was calling her to do. Mary started to do charity work as many society wives do, but she went well beyond the cursory interest or thoughtful gesture. Aiding the poor, the sick, and the disadvantaged, Mary found a way to get involved not just by donating money but by rolling up her sleeves. At the suggestion of her brother who was helping out with missionary work in then war-torn Korea, she spearheaded relief efforts by convincing ships in the port of Los Angeles heading to Korea to carry care packages. Then she mobilized thousands in Hollywood to donate. When her nephew was diagnosed with leukemia, she learned of the amazing efforts to help children at the City of Hope hospital in California. She immediately began mobilizing support for the hospital, convincing toy companies like Mattel and Hasbro to donate thousands of toys and convincing See's Candy to deluge the hospital with sweet treats. She even convinced Marlon Brando to pay a visit to the hospital one Christmas, and he became a longtime supporter. The list of her efforts and successes goes on.

She still wanted to do more. Meanwhile, she and her husband grew further and further apart, as he took more and more business trips, and she did more and more charity work. By the time she was forty-five, they were so divergent in their views of the world and their marriage that they hardly communicated with each other at all.

When a priest heard of her efforts with the poor, he asked her to come to Tijuana to help bring supplies. There she encountered La Mesa Penitentiary. She was struck by the dire state of the prison, where inmates were deprived of the most basic needs like toothbrushes and dental care, blankets and eyeglasses. She began making regular visits, driving three hours each way to bring supplies and help however she could.

As her commitment to the poor and the oppressed grew, her husband's dissatisfaction with it did too. In 1972, he moved out. At age forty-five, with her children grown up, and with no more burdens of a marriage that was not sanctioned by the Church, Mary felt drawn back to the Church. She suddenly had a tremendous yearning to receive communion and to attend services, something that she had not done in years. She spent more and more time in solitude in a beach house on the California coast north of Los Angeles. There she would spend hours walking the beach, reflecting. The rest of her time was spent doing what she loved most, helping the poor and disadvantaged in whatever she could.

Finally she realized what she was called to do was right in front of her. She wanted to help the underprivileged and renew her faith. So one day, she put on a homemade habit and moved to a prison cell in La Mesa Penitentiary. Since 1977, she has lived there in one of the roughest prisons in Mexico in a tiny 10-by-10 foot concrete cell where she spiritually counsels and supports 2,500 male and female prisoners.

Now known as Mother Antonia, she counsels the worst of the worst of Mexico's criminals because she believes in the goodness of all people, including murderers. When she was fifty, she took her vows as a missionary sister and officially founded the Eudist Servants of the Eleventh Hour, an order of nuns who enter religious life later in their lives, after having other careers or raising families.

At the time of this writing, she is eighty-one and is battling a serious heart condition. Even so, the tiny five-feet-two nun risks her life on a routine basis to help quell prison riots, visit lepers, and wash and prepare the bodies of the unidentified who die alone. She ministers to the most vile offenders and brutal prison guards. She comforts as best as she can bringing everything from kind words to dentists to work on the prisoners for free. All the while, she does it with a song in her heart and a smile on her face. Pope John Paul II and Mother Theresa both recognized her for her extraordinary mission, calling her the "Prison Angel," the same as the name of the book written about her in 2005 by Pulitzer Prize–winning authors Mary Jordan and Kevin Sullivan.

Mary did not know that any of this would happen when her two marriages failed. She knew only that she had to keep going and keeping on, and that she needed to find meaning and direction within the events of those marriages that could inspire and motivate her to love. Though this initially led her to reconsider the characteristics of her husbands, soon it led her deeper to understand herself, who she was, and what God wanted her to do. And that led her to consider her true calling.

In the Beginning: Loneliness

God is not always on *our* time schedule when it comes to matters of the heart, but he is always on target! If that is our mindset, then love will happen quite naturally without the need for desperation. Desperation is a deadly disease that breaks the heart and kills the spirit by reducing us to our base physical instincts and superficial needs. The most dangerous place of all for that desperation to rear its ugly head is in the arena of romantic love.

A steady diet of infatuated desperation abounds in our movies through characters who want only to satisfy their physical desires for companionship as quickly as possible, and in the sensory overload of television turning us into immediate-gratification addicts incapable of patience, abstinence, and thoughtful living.

All this leads so many of us to throw ourselves thoughtlessly and heartlessly headlong into doomed relationships in the name of romance. In actuality, it is desperation that is motivating us through a popular cultural message that preaches, "Find a mate now!" or else we are lost.

Ads for dating services, matchmaker Internet Web sites, and the like proliferate as entrepreneurs desperate for money promise us the perfect mate, as if there were such a thing. More important, they mislead us to believe that love is something we can order up, then shape and mold into exactly what we want it to be.

In contrast, allowing God into our lives by living a respectful, faithfully dutiful, and full life, then opening our heads and our hearts to who he sends our way seems implausible, unsuccessful, and way too much work. Yet in the end, we are willing to expend a whole lot of effort hunting for our mate, then trying to force something to happen with the ones we catch.

Loneliness can be a powerful depressant, especially in our increasingly impersonal and detached society. With people moving constantly from one end of the country, and the world for that matter, to the other, the usual companions that might normally comfort single people, namely, old friends and family, are not as readily available, pushing many people to prematurely choose a lover and a mate. Furthermore, there are a hundred other reasons that psychologists tell us why we may feel the "need" to be in a relationship, and one of the most dangerous is because for some it can distract us from dealing with many of our personal issues.

Ultimately, we may be so busy looking for love that we are blind to God's gift of love when it actually arrives. Open your heart to those the Lord sends your way while you are doing his work.

This is especially meaningful for those that wait until later in life to settle down, or those that have been catapulted by circumstances into looking for a mate later in life. This state of being single is a real blessing but we must learn to embrace it and to appreciate it. Though many see being alone as a catastrophe that could have no possible worth, that is contrary to the experiences of so many that have waited for one reason or another for love.

Did not Christ tell his disciples to leave their families to follow him? As difficult as it may be to embrace that solitude, we do not need to yield to the compulsion, or expectation, to jump headfirst into relationships. At times in our lives, solitude is exactly what we need to do in order to hear God's call for our direction. Take the time to get to know yourself before you try to present that self to someone else. For how can you know *who* is right for you, if you do not know *what* is right for you?

6
Abandoning Perfection
Illness

Why do many feel so discouraged by illness, from the simplest of colds to the most serious cancers? Have we become so acclimated to a view of reality that says we are machines that either function correctly or incorrectly? If we cannot function at our optimum level, then why even bother to go on?

What if there is some greater meaning and purpose in being less than tip-top shape? The Bible may be right when it says, "To every thing there is a season, and a time to every matter under the heaven" (Eccl 3:1).

Could there actually be a purpose in illness, wisdom in weakness, and clarity in confused thinking? Could there actually be a time for illness?

Learning from Others

The late, great Pope John Paul II was criticized over the last years of his papacy for choosing not to resign from office despite his progressive Parkinson's disease. The reason for his decision, he said repeatedly, was to demonstrate the experience of illness and its meaning to a world that had become less and less accepting of human imperfection, frailty, and vulnerability.

During World War II, the Nazis came up with the insane idea of a "master race." A master race did not leave room for anything short of perfection, as if that were possible. Though we have all heard the horrific stories of the ghastly atrocities inflicted upon the Jews, there is less written about the abuse and murder of the sick, the mentally ill, and the physically challenged. The Nazis believed that these "dysfunctional" people polluted the gene pool with their weakness and imperfection. Today, we are thankfully free of the methods of those atrocities. However, are we in danger of dismissing the value of life through many of our other practices and beliefs that dismiss the value of those who are ill and of illness itself?

Life has many purposes and many values in many forms, some of which none of us can know. Illness is an extraordinarily powerful opportunity to see and to realize some of those less-obvious purposes and values if we embrace it once we have succumbed to it. There is probably no greater representation of the old adage "God works in mysterious ways."

Keith was a happily married husband and father who had been in a horrible head-on collision while coming home from work one sunny California afternoon. He was rushed to the hospital in time to save his life, but the force of the impact caused serious brain damage. His condition was declared hopeless. Doctors insisted that even if by some miracle he ever emerged from his comalike state, he would never have any real quality of life. He would never again be able to walk, talk, speak, or even swallow on his own. Doctors recommended removing his feeding tube and when he went into cardiac arrest, letting him die.

His loving wife Marilyn refused to hear of such things. She was relentlessly hopeful, as one might expect any loving spouse would be. She was not about to stop fighting for him, the man she loved, the man who had always fought for her for so many years before the accident. Every day she sat by his side for hours, speaking lovingly to him as he lingered in his hospital bed. Meanwhile she did everything she could think of to bring him back. She read book after book about his condition and tried in vain to stimulate his senses.

She prayed and begged God for a sign. No matter how much faith she had, nothing worked. Days dragged into weeks, then into months, and all the while doctors were pressuring her to end Keith's life by removing the life-nourishing feeding tubes and IVs.

She refused. One day she was sifting through a box of old pictures of the couple together in happier times. When she came across a picture of them at their summer cottage, on a second honeymoon, embracing for the camera, she shared it with her husband. To her amazement, when she held up the picture to him, he suddenly raised his arm and reached out for it. Then just like that, he returned to his unresponsive state.

Now convinced that Keith was alive and aware inside, Marilyn stepped up efforts to bring him back. She tried raising his hands to make him brush his own teeth, putting a pen in his hand and asking him to write letters, anything to solicit another response. A few weeks later when she placed a comb in his hair, he suddenly reached up and grabbed it and began combing his own hair. This time he stayed around to see how it looked in a mirror.

Her husband was back. It would take him years to be rehabilitated to a functional state but she stayed loyal to him through it all. Being there to save her husband was life-changing to say the least for Keith's wife. As for Keith, his experience is a compelling argument for why we should never give up on our loved ones, even when doctors tell us there is no hope, and why we should not give up on ourselves either when illness gets us down.

Healing Ourselves:
The Challenge of Illness

We see that new view only if we open our eyes to the positive potential of illness, which is not really consistent with our perfectionist culture. Presumably, none of us wants to be sick or injured, and we should try everything we can to maintain our health. But when all those efforts fail, there is a lesson to be learned, action to be taken, and counseling to be accepted. Why we are hiding and what we are afraid of are real matters of the heart and head to consider.

Sometimes illnesses can arise from deep-seated subconscious fears, anxieties, and anger. We can keep these emotions and feelings so buried inside of us that we do not even realize they are there—that is, until our bodies give way to the constant anguish. When that happens, we are suddenly overcome with illness, and we cannot begin to figure out why. Countless books have been written about coming to terms with the root internal causes of many stress related and psychologically related ailments. But responding to the illness in a positive way can yield value and potential benefit, rather than letting it drag you down. Especially, since value is the last thing most people are thinking about when they get sick. Most of us just feel miserable and are often unable to think about anything positive.

That certainly was the last thing that Holly was thinking about when her body suddenly shut down on her when she was only twenty-eight years old. A superactive athlete and a competitive cyclist who usually biked fifty or sixty miles a week, she collapsed a few miles into a race for no apparent reason.

She was physically exhausted, her abdomen was wracked with pain, and she could not get herself out of bed for two days.

When she finally had enough strength to get herself to the doctor a week later, the news was not good. She was diagnosed with ulcerative colitis, which is a technical way of explaining that two-and-a-half feet of her intestines were bleeding, and it was killing her, both figuratively and literally. The disease, similar to Crohn's, is a substantial inflammation and ulceration of the large intestine, which results in decreased absorption of nutrients and weakening of the body. Such inflammations can also lead to a series of degenerative diseases including cancer. *"The doctor told me this was a chronic illness, that was never going to go away,"* recalled Holly. *"And I would need to be on medication if I wanted to live."* Actually it was six different medications she would need, every day for the rest of her life.

Not feeling she had much of a choice, Holly took the pills. Within two weeks she was so weak from the medication that facing the effects of the disease itself almost seemed a better alternative. *"I couldn't eat anything, I was bruising all over, and I was losing my hair,"* revealed Holly. *"I felt worse than I did before. This was not a solution."*

Holly told the doctor she did not want to take the pills anymore, and he told her it was either that or surgery. Unwilling to accept living the rest of her life dependent on drugs and not at all interested in having her body carved into pieces, she enlisted the help of a naturopathic clinic. There she found alternative treatments and immediately began to see results. The clinic first prescribed a combination of vitamins and fish proteins to which her body responded positively. Then she was tested for food allergies, of which she had many. The most effective treatment was deep tissue manipulation, in which a doctor massaged toxins from her body. At this point, Holly learned that there was a whole lot more than toxins that she was holding in.

"I felt all this anger inside me every time they would press down there," said Holly. *"I was tightening up, and I couldn't let go. But I didn't know why."*

What was she angry about? She found out one day when the doctor pressed on a particular pressure point in her abdomen, sending a jolt of incredible pain through her entire body and an arrow through her heart as it inspired a painful memory. *"I had this flashback of my dad telling me I was a failure after losing a soccer game,"* explains Holly. *"As soon as that happened, I felt all the pain go away."*

Within a few months, her treatments brought back a flood of unresolved memories. *"I played the piano for eighteen years. After the best recital I ever had, he said I played the piece too slow and I picked the wrong song,"* revealed Holly. *"Nothing I could do was ever good enough for him. He could never even tell me he loved me."*

Holly now believed that the inflammation in her bowel resulted from her subconscious anger at and resentment of her father, and that the problem would not go away until she faced it head-on.

"I realized I could accept the situation I was born into and respond to it positively instead of being angry about it," said Holly. *"I had a father that couldn't show love, because his mother was never able to show him love. So I could help him adjust. I decided to teach him how to hug. I knew it wasn't my responsibility to teach him how to love, but it was a lot more constructive than spending the rest of my life upset about it."*

She also realized that she was too sensitive to her father's rejection. Such sensitivity was not limited to her father either. *"I was very affected by how people treated me,"* said Holly. *"Every little thing had a tremendous impact on me, and I knew that needed to change. I couldn't keep going through life that way."*

Amazingly, as soon as Holly realized this, her physical recovery began. She stopped feeling the pain in six months without medication. A year later she was eating normally and a year and a half later, she climbed back on a bike.

Then one day Holly threw out all the books and information she had accumulated over the two years since her collapse. *"I was finally ready to leave it behind and move on,"* she declared. *"Only now I had all the tools inside to deal with my dad, my life, and everything. I'll always be sensitive, but now I have the awareness and the perspective to process that constructively. But none of that would have ever happened if it hadn't been for my collapse."*

A few years later Holly was the picture of health and happiness, beaming with confidence and excitement about life and love. She overcame so much more than her illness.

The "Ultimate Cure-All" Does Not Exist!

Holly obviously needed to deal with her illness for a reason. If she avoided dealing with it or just took prescribed medications, she might not even be around today to tell her story, or at the least not in the highly evolved and healthy state she is in.

Yet, that is exactly what seems to happen to many of us in our pragmatist and perfectionist society. Our popular culture is inundated with quick fixes for every medical ailment you can think of. Instead of dealing with the reasons for all this illness and our challenges, we run away to drugs that will make the problem go away. Meanwhile our bodies, minds, and souls continue to be plagued by the same demons and diseases day after day until finally that one tragic day when the pills do not work anymore and our lives fall apart.

In a perfectionist society, there is no room for failure. In such a society, illness, whether mental or physical, is a sign of failure rather than an impetus for growth and grace. However, in a

Christian environment, or any philosophically compassionate culture, illness can and should be a purposeful and meaningful motivator rather than a demerit. The illness is there for a reason. Whether it signals a need for a change, or simply a need for a rest and reevaluation of our lives, it has value and can bring grace and blessings. The body and the mind are signaling some need, and confronting that need can bring about many personality adjustments and a great deal of personal growth.

The Blessing of Illness: To Heal for Others

Personal growth comes in many forms and leads to different blessings for you and for all around you. Illness makes us reach out to others *for* help and *to* help. It humbles us in many ways, yet it toughens us in other ways.

The concept of our own bodies attacking us is not only debilitating physically but emotionally devastating and downright terrifying. It is there in that low place where you can receive some of the greatest gifts that life could offer, and where you sometimes find the greatest gifts that you can offer to the world around you. Because as soon as illness forces you to look away from your own perceived greatness, it is amazing how great you can really become as you reach out to do whatever you can to love others. The humility illness brings often leads us to stop caring so much about ourselves and worry more about how others are being affected by our illness. In fact, sometimes that is what actually gets us well. That love acts like medicine as it flows through our heads, hearts, and bodies, and we are overcome by altruistic strength we never knew we had.

Giving into the compulsions to love and be loved are both at the forefront of understanding and of constructively embracing our illness. When we are mired in one of the toughest battles of our life, the fight to survive, we are often inspired to love more totally and more meaningfully than we ever have, than we ever knew, we could. This love is so transforming it actually can inspire our own healing, especially when it reaches out and solicits love in return, the love we need so badly when overcome by illness.

Rosemarie was a fifty-seven-year-old mother who found a lump in her breast. She went to the doctor and her worst fears were confirmed. It was cancer caused by years of smoking. She was scared, but her amazing love and dedication to her children were so strong, they endowed her with incredible strength and fortitude to face her illness, something that eventually helped her to overcome the greatest of odds.

Even when she first learned of her illness, she was more concerned with her two grown children, Anthony and Cathy, than herself. Just a few years earlier, their father died very unexpectedly of a massive heart attack that he suffered on the way to work. Now the last thing she wanted to tell them was what she was facing. *"They had been through so much with their father, and I didn't want to worry them,"* explained Rosemarie. *"So I was there all alone at the doctor's when I got the news."*

She was confident she could face this without burdening her children, partly because she had faced illness before. She contracted polio when she was three years old and was quarantined in a Catholic hospital. She spent three years there, bedridden in a full-body cast. If she could handle that, she figured she could handle this. *"I always had a very deep faith in God that pulled me through a lot,"* explained Rosemarie. *"So as scared as I was, I knew he would be there for me."*

Despite her efforts to keep the cancer to herself, her children found out when her daughter spied a note for a doctor's appointment on her mother's refrigerator. *"They were so worried and got so involved right away,"* remembered Rosemarie. *"I was glad they cared so much, but I didn't want to disrupt their lives or see them that upset."*

A few weeks later Rosemarie had the lump successfully removed. A routine X-ray revealed something else on her lung. After a CAT scan, the doctors assured her that there was nothing to worry about, and that she should go home and come back in a few months for a check-up. Her concerned children convinced Rosemarie to go to the renowned Sloan Kettering Cancer Center in New York City. A battery of tests revealed a shocking diagnosis: cancer had eaten away a third of her lung. Rosemarie was terrified, but still she never broke down in front of her children. *"This was all happening so fast that I was really starting to fall apart,"* revealed Rosemarie. *"But I didn't want the kids to see that. I knew I needed to stay strong for them."*

Wanting to protect them, Rosemarie continually asked her children not to worry themselves with her situation. When they insisted, she accepted their help. *"I didn't want to unload this problem onto their shoulders,"* explained Rosemarie. *"But on the other hand, I thought if doing something to help would make them feel better, then I didn't want to stop that either."*

Together they all faced the unavoidable reality—the bottom third of her lung needed to be removed immediately. As Rosemarie and her children prepared for the massive operation, incredibly, she found another lump on her breast. It had been growing out of control since the first operation, and somehow the doctor who performed the surgery never found it. Now there was no choice but to perform both the lung surgery and a mastectomy at the same time. The chances of surviving lung cancer alone were extremely low. Surviving two cancers and two surgeries at once was practically unheard of. The doctors told her children they did not think she would make it. Despite all the positive energy she could muster, the horrible disease was finally beginning to take its toll on Rosemarie's spirit. *"That's when I really reached my breaking point,"* she explained. *"I told my kids that if they find anything else, I'm not having it taken out. Whatever happens will happen."*

After the lengthy six-hour surgery, Rosemarie woke up in a hospital bed with her children at her side. Her body ravaged by the double-surgery, with tubes sticking out of her everywhere, she felt and looked like she was at death's door. *"I still remember the horrible look on Anthony's face when he saw me like that,"* said Rosemarie. *"I realized how awful I must have looked, and I knew it was really killing him to see me like that. I hated making him hurt like that."* The next day, when she forced herself to her feet to take a stroll down the hall of the hospital, what she saw affected her even more. *"It was like a warehouse filled with people dying of cancer,"* recounted Rosemarie. *"There were so many that were worse off than me and their families crying. I didn't want that to ever be my children."*

The mere thought of causing her children that kind of pain made her determined to get back on her feet for the sake of her family. *"Before the operation I said to myself that if God wants me to be here, then I'll open my eyes,"* recalled Rosemarie. *"He was there for me. Now what right did I have to feel sorry for myself? God kept me around for a reason. Maybe it was to inspire others. Whatever it was, I knew I didn't ever want to see that look on my son's face ever again."*

The next day, still wracked with pain, she fixed her hair, did her makeup, and spruced herself up so she would not look so sick when her children came to visit. *"When Anthony saw me I think he must have been shocked,"* said Rosemarie. *"He couldn't believe how much better I seemed. I felt terrible, but I didn't want him to know that."*

She survived the surgery but she still had to survive lung cancer. Doing that meant giving up her lifelong tobacco habit, something she thought was going to be very difficult. Once again her concern for her children made it easier than she thought. *"I never had any desire to smoke again because I knew that if they saw me revert back to smoking, it would really hurt them after all they had been through with me,"* she explained. *"How could I do that to them? I could never put them through that again. Before the surgery, I prayed to God for the strength to quit after the operation. I guess he answered that prayer through my children."*

Rosemarie rebounded and recovered from her surgery in record time. She was not only back on her feet but back at work only a few months after the second surgery. Doctors could not understand how she recovered as well and as fast as she did, but Rosemarie knew. *"After my first surgery, my daughter broke down crying at the coffee table with me, and she told me that she didn't want me to die,"* she explained. *"I promised her that I wasn't going anywhere. I knew neither one of my children could bear the thought of losing me. I know that had a lot to do with me recovering so quickly. Thank God, he gave me the strength to do it."*

Twelve years later, she is still cancer-free. Rosemarie tries to use her experience to inspire and encourage her family and anyone else facing tough times. *"Anytime Anthony or Cathy is down, I tell them to look at me and what I made it through,"* said Rosemarie. *"When I hear that someone is sick or has cancer, I try to let them know what I went through and that they can make it too. I am so grateful to God for that second chance. I know that he kept me around for a reason."*

Divine Detours

Illness can inspire us by reminding us how important we are to our loved ones and how much they need us to get well. It can also put us in a strange and uncomfortable place, one that makes us depend on others and open up to people and ideas in ways that we never thought we might possible. More often than not, we also learn along the way what our loved ones mean to us and how devoted they are. Though we would never wish to be in that situation, the love and devotion of those closest to us can be transforming.

Even with love and support, it is certainly not easy being sick, and anyone who has ever faced illness knows that. We never know what will be asked of us and how we will need to deal with the hardships that it brings. However, the humbling, the reaching out and reaching in, the metamorphosis that occurs is a painful process that breaks you down and makes you rebuild from the inside out. All the good, the love, the power that will come after enduring that experience is extraordinary.

The story of Karen Smyers is a stunning example of somebody forced to dig deeper than she ever thought she would have to, not just to overcome the most unlikely string of injuries, but to perform at the highest physical level imaginable while doing so. When we talk about people doing the legwork, the "Sixth Step to Serenity," there is no more-apt example.

Karen is a world-renowned triathlete who burst onto the scene as an amateur in the 1980s and won her first championship in 1990, a record-breaking victory in the famed Ironman event in Kona, Hawaii, in 1995. She was on track for the 2000 Olympics but her carefree life turned into a tragedy in 1997. A career-threatening leg injury, getting hit by a truck, and battling thyroid cancer were just a few obstacles that the forty-five-year-old champion endured along the way to becoming one of the oldest champion triathletes in the sport's history. When she discussed her storied career, it was clear that she had an entirely different perspective on winning, being successful, and dealing with illness, injuries, and life in general than most modern-day athletes, a perspective that made possible the greatest joys life could ever offer. *"It made me see my performance goals differently,"* explained Karen. *"I realized how much I loved competing and that just getting to the starting line is sometimes a blessing. I looked at all those hurdles as opportunities for growth or a chance to try something new in my life."*

As a child, Karen once complained to her mother that she was going to fail her swim class because she could not do a frog kick. *"My mother said, 'That's OK. You'll just do it over next year. Eventually you'll get it,'"* recalls Karen.

It took Karen three years to *get it.* She went on to become a breast-stroke champion in college. More importantly, her parent's loving and accepting perspective on hardships and obstacles was a big part of what got her through some of the most harrowing and challenging times of her life.

Two weeks before defending her Ironman championship, and in the best shape of her life, she was taking down storm windows in her New England home when the glass suddenly shattered. A shard shot straight through her calf like a bullet, splitting open her hamstring muscle. The pain was so intense Karen struggled to stay conscious to dial 911.

Karen was sidelined for a year. She thought about how she could use the down time constructively. She decided to have a baby. *"I figured I had to find something that I didn't need my hamstring for,"* she joked. *"Before the accident, taking a year off from my training and going through the physical changes of having a baby would be scary. But now I had a chance and a reason to do it. Taking the time off took the pressure off my rehab too. I had something else to do."*

As if it was meant to be, she conceived almost immediately. Nine months later, after forty-eight hours of labor and a C-section, she delivered a healthy baby girl, which she named Jenna.

Amazingly, she raced again only two months later. Karen took on the world at the Goodwill Games in New York. However, the hamstring injury still hampered her performance. *"I got smoked,"* admits Karen. *"I didn't finish last but I was pretty close."*

For a champion used to winning, it was not easy to take. It changed the way she looked at racing for the rest of her career. *"I had to dig down deep to finish that race even though I knew I wasn't going to come close to winning it. That's when I made a promise to myself that I wouldn't ever judge myself by where I placed. I realized I loved this sport, and it was so gratifying for me to be able to participate in it, especially after being prevented from doing so for a year. From then on I told myself I would just do the best that I could."*

She set her mind on the future and returning to the Ironman in Hawaii the next year. Training day and night, Karen was in top form again before the competition in August of 1998. Then one day during her cycling workout, as she headed onto a narrow country road, suddenly she heard the ominous roar of an eighteen-wheeler trying to pass. As the road took a turn, so did the truck, right into Karen, sending her back to the hospital with six broken ribs, a separated shoulder, and a lung contusion.

Once again it was time away from racing. *"There just wasn't much you could do at that point but wait and heal,"* explained Karen. *"It gave me a lot of time to think about things. The emotional scars of being hit from behind by a truck were actually harder to overcome than the physical injuries."*

She remembered the promise she made after her hamstring injury and why she was doing this in the first place. *"I realized I wanted to keep going,"* revealed Karen, *"not for the money, but because this sport made me happy and gratified me."*

Amazing critics and commentators, Karen was back on her feet by the next year in time to make a run for the Sydney Olympics in 2000. She was in the running for the team, but she was way behind her colleagues in points and training. She entered as many major races as she could to make up for it and she kept winning.

First she took the Pan Am Games Qualifier race at the St. Anthony's Triathlon in Florida, then the St. Croix International, finally being recognized as the U.S. Olympic Committee's Triathlete of the Year. To close out the competitive year, she scored an impressive second place in Ironman, losing only to a record-setting winner.

Unbelievably, tragedy struck again. Three weeks after Ironman, during the last race of the season, a pedal fell off the bike in front of Karen's, forcing the rider to lose control and careen into her. She was out of the race and in the hospital with a broken collarbone. Then doctors noticed some abnormal nodules on her neck. They did a biopsy and discovered the thirty-eight-year-old champion had thyroid cancer. *"How could I possibly have cancer?"* she recalled saying. *"I just placed second in an Ironman."*

A six-hour surgery removed much of the tumor. She still needed radiation treatment, and she feared that the treatments would weaken her too much to compete in the Olympic trials. After doctors assured her it would in no way threaten her long-term chances, Karen decided to delay them.

The disease and surgery already took their toll on her conditioning. She could not overtake the field of world-class athletes at the top of their game. Karen missed the cut. Though disappointed, she took it in stride. *"For many athletes the Olympics was the Holy Grail,"* she said. *"But for me it was just the trying that was important."*

Another surgery and the radiation treatment meant competing was out for the rest of the year. After tests showed the cancer had been eradicated, she bounced back again the very next year in 2001 to win five races, including her seventh National Champion title. She even returned to the Ironman at forty years old to take fifth place.

She took the next year off to have another baby but a miscarriage dashed her dreams. With that year's Ironman only a few days away, she thought competing might help take her mind off the misfortune, and doctors gave their approbation.

However, half-way through the race, Karen broke down with incredible shooting pain in her abdomen. She feared the worst—that it was connected to her miscarriage. When doctors assured her it was unrelated, she trudged on, determined to finish, no matter how long it took. *"My goal had completely changed at that point,"* said Karen. *"It wasn't about winning at all anymore."*

If she quit, she could avoid the embarrassment of coming in so far behind in a race she figured to win. As the day dragged into night, Karen slowly but surely made her way to the finish line, making small but meaningful strides along the way. *"I kept changing my goals and making a new plan,"* recalled Karen. *"First it was just about being able to walk. Then it was about seeing if I could run a little. Then it was catching up to my sister who was also running. I figured we could cross the finish line together."*

It was not pretty, but Karen slumped across the finish line late that evening. *"When you're running a race and you're winning, it's easy to keep going,"* said Karen. *"When you know you don't have a chance, it really takes discipline. But you can't just quit because your pride is hurt. Telling yourself just to do your best takes the pressure off by taking away the anxiety of an outcome-based perspective. I told myself years before that it didn't matter where I placed. Now I really proved that I believed it."*

Karen's medical mishaps would have been enough to make most people give up, but her perspective on them allowed her to reap insights and blessings in her life. All of that kept her going in real life, as well as in racing, to endure the worst and find the best. She enjoyed the experience of giving birth to her second child, Casey, in 2004.

She returned to racing that same year to come in twentieth in the Ironman in 2004 and then in the Top 10 in 2005 at forty-three years old.

Contagious Compassion

Just as illness helps us acknowledge the need to love and be loved, it helps us affirm those loving relationships with God and others that are already present in our life. We can see our illness as an opportunity to love others and to depend on our values to get us through adversity. They may be opportunities to validate our beliefs and our strength rather than diminish them. Karen saw tragedy as an opportunity to be a mother, to find contentment in her best efforts and her love of competition, and to appreciate the great gifts God gave her to compete.

Illness can be a total validation of the faithful life that you have always lived. When you need it most, the fruits of that lifestyle come back to nourish and support you. It gives you the opportunity to confirm your commitment to that way of life and to pass it on to others, so it spreads like wildfire transforming others and passing along God's grace in many different ways.

When I was covering celebrities as an entertainment reporter for the tabloids and then *People* magazine, I realized many stars actually were their stereotype—totally self-absorbed and egocentric. However, I met a legendary star who treated me and people in general with the utmost respect, even though he had spent years as one of Hollywood's highest-paid entertainers. He was a man of faith and character, traits that earned him the love and respect of many, and which served him well when he found himself facing the ultimate obstacle.

Comic and crooner, Jim Nabors first hit the big time as the humble, half-witted country-bumpkin mechanic on the *Andy Griffith Show* in the early sixties. The character, which Nabors concocted himself, was a comical compilation of folks the Alabama native encountered in his youth. He parlayed that small role into a starring one on his own extraordinarily successful sit-com in 1964, *Gomer Pyle U.S.M.C.* The hit show about a bumbling but goodhearted marine shot to the top of the ratings overnight, where it stayed throughout the sixties. The show spawned another hugely successful and lucrative career for Nabors as a recording artist with his wholesome repertoire of old traditional standards and gospel favorites. His all-around talents even earned him his own top-rated variety show in 1969 on CBS, the *Jim Nabors Hour*.

Continually in front of the camera, Nabors became a household name. Behind it, he became one of the most beloved and popular stars in Hollywood, known for being one of those few-and-far-between real people who made it because of real talent and real character, without ever succumbing to Hollywood attitude and arrogance. In a town known for opportunism and backstabbing, he was a noble man who never put fame over friends, family, or personal integrity. He always respected his fans, personally answering many fan letters himself.

In his sixties, a trip to Asia left him feeling lethargic and worn out. Blood tests revealed he had hepatitis B. Worse still, his liver was already seriously damaged and he was dying. *"They basically told me I didn't have a chance,"* recalled Nabors. *"At my worst point I had lost sixty or seventy pounds and I was so sick they thought a liver transplant wouldn't even work because my body would reject it."*

The man who had always been there for his friends got a little positive payback. Best friend and legendary star Carol Burnett was determined to get her pal back on his feet. *"She researched and read everything she could about my condition,"* revealed Nabors. *"Then she found out about a transplant program at UCLA where they were using some pretty effective drugs to suppress the transplant rejection in very bad cases like mine, and it was working. So she got me into the program, and before I knew it I was on the list to get a transplant."*

Still, Nabors was in a precarious physical condition until a liver was available. While he waited, he grew sicker and sicker. At his lowest point, doctors told him he had only a week left to live but the faith he spent a lifetime developing now comforted him. *"It humbles you to be told that you're that close to finishing out your life,"* revealed Nabors. *"But I couldn't in good conscience pray for a transplant because you know that somebody has to die to make that possible. So I said, God, it's in your hands."*

Then the good news came—the organ that would save his life was available. The surgery was a success and Nabors came back strong and fast, healthy enough to resume his career. Only a few months after the horrific ordeal, accompanied by his friend Carol Burnett, he sang "The Impossible Dream" to a sea of fellow transplant recipients at a special event at the hospital that saved his life.

Nabors' success was a tremendous validation of his lifestyle, standing by his family and friends all those years. Mr. Nabors was a breath of fresh air. He was so genuine, kind, and respectful that it turned my darkening heart a little brighter. Nabors' kindness and sincerity, his integrity, and his openness to me inspired a young reporter at the time with whom he agreed to speak to about his ordeal.

After the surgery I bought him a Bible to thank him, and his heartfelt appreciation touched an even deeper chord in me. It made me realize God wanted me to do something better and nobler than chase celebrities around.

7

When the World Stops
Money Problems

If money makes the world go around, what happens when you
lose it all? If value is measured only in temporal or material
worth, when does life itself become worthless? There is an alternative view that alleviates a great deal of the pain and suffering
that an obsession with money and its loss brings, and it is staring
us right in the face.

While consoling a depressed colleague recently, I realized
just how revolutionary and liberating the Christian idea of money
is, but how easily it is replaced by temporal ideas, even by so-
called Christians. My friend was totally demoralized because he
had lost a job he hated, even though he found a new job he loved
that made a whole lot less money. This person is not someone
you would call materialistic. He and his family live frugally. He is
a loving and devoted father and husband, who did not like his
former position as a liquor sales rep because it took him on the
road too often, away from his family. He did not want to wake up
one day ten years from now to see his children grown before he
ever got the chance to see them grow. Plus, the job involved a lot
of drinking and general misbehaving that did not suit his marriage. Getting laid off was the best thing that ever happened to
him, and he was still making enough to pay the bills. Yet, this

incredibly caring and devoted guy who is so rich with his family's love was lamenting to me like a failure. Why?

The problem is that he could not kick the habit we have in modern society of gauging our success by how much we make. "Money is the root of all evil" sounds great in a Sunday sermon, but how realistic is it?

Christ showed us that happiness and success are not derived from what we get but, on the contrary, from what we give. In parable after parable, he referred to the transitory worth of money: He endorsed the paying of taxes by citing the face of Caesar on the coins, thereby signaling that Caesar, not the people, owned the coins (Matt 22:21). He also told the rich young ruler to give all his money and his belongings away (Matt 19:16–21).

If we use our faith and the innately valuable self-image it offers, we are freed from the chains of monetary madness. Then we do not need to try to serve two masters, viewing our success as the fulfillment of worldly desires, or while simultaneously trying to assimilate and exemplify the lessons, love, and value-added (to borrow a chic advertising term) life of Christ. Trying to do both would be like trying to fit an elephant though the eye of a needle.

"Money for Love" vs. "Love for Money"

Every year millions of people in this country gamble on the lottery in the hopes of hitting it big. Few of them do. The biggest losers are actually many of those that do. The fact is that many lottery winners of huge amounts wind up bankrupt within a few years, their lives coming apart at the seams.

Mack Metcalf and his wife Virginia Merida won $34 million back in 2000. Just three years later, after his life spiraled completely out of control, Mack dropped dead at forty-five of the complications of alcoholism. His wife was found dead in her bed of a possible drug overdose, the day before Thanksgiving that same year. In the interim, they lost their money on a host of extravagances, from expensive horses and vintage automobiles to luxurious houses. After he won, Mack's past came back like a bad check as angry exwives and abandoned children sought out him and his money. Poor decisions and bad relationships piled up over the next three years, as a lifetime of bad blood took its toll on him and his wife. *"Any problems people have, money magnifies it so much, it's unbelievable,"* said Robert Merida, one of Ms. Merida's three brothers.[1] Mack's first wife echoed those sentiments. *"If he hadn't won, he would have worked like regular people and maybe had twenty years left,"* said Marilyn Collins. *"But when you put that kind of money in the hands of somebody with problems, it just helps them kill themselves."*[2]

Many of the lottery winners in this country have fared similar fates, either completely squandering their winnings or throwing away their lives through a series of bad decisions that exemplified the same misbegotten notion of money they had before they won the lottery. Now, obviously not everyone who plays the lottery thinks like this. Some winners have been very wise and very thoughtful about how they spent their money. Perhaps, many of those who compulsively play the lottery see money as the "end-all and be-all." When the Bible says money is the root of all evil, it does not mean money itself is evil—it is the obsession with money, the belief that it is more important than people, the people you are willing to betray or abandon to get it or to keep it. Or that it is more important than morality, the morality you will forgo to have it.

When you place all your faith in money like that, and you lose it all, what have you got? You wind up with what you started with—an empty soul and an empty life.

None of us need nor can afford to live a life of complete austerity, rejecting all worldly goods and concerns. Christ never said that. Quite contrarily, he spent more than a few words telling the apostles how to catch all those fish and about getting our "daily bread" in the Lord's Prayer.

God wants and needs us to make money in order to care for ourselves, our families, our communities, and those who fall between the cracks because of health or circumstance. Money should not be accumulated for the sake of power but spent to do good works. It is how we make it and how we spend it, as a sacramental gift from God to be used for God's intentions, that is most important. In this perspective, money has no inherent power to control us; it is simply a tool. The only way to truly derive joy from material items is because we know we achieved them through loving others or are using them to show or extend our love to others.

When we lose money, ultimately it is *that* attitude and perspective that drives those individuals who rebound best. Should we lose those things or that means of living, though we will obviously be affected, we will still have all the love and support of and for those people that were there before and still are.

When the Chips Are Gone!

Once we change our perspective on money so that we view it as a byproduct of living a life of love, something different occurs when depositing our check: we feel a contentment and happiness that no money can buy. Even if we lose all the money, we still have that happiness since we still have all the love and the loved ones that this attitude and way of life produced. It completely changes our view of financial ruin and financial success.

When monetary hardship confronts us, it actually can inspire us by highlighting that enlightenment.

Roy Rinard of Oregon had worked for Portland Gas and Electric, a subsidiary of Enron, for over twenty-two years as a lineman, pushing his body to the limit climbing poles in the cold and the rain of the Pacific Northwest. He commonly worked sixty-hour weeks so he could put away enough money to retire when he was sixty-two, because that was about as long as he figured his body would hold out at such a tough job. At fifty-three, he was heading toward fulfilling his dream in 2001. That is when Enron imploded after a series of shady deals, mismanagement, inflated profit reports, and fraudulent transactions.

Roy lost nearly $600,000 in a flash. Worse still, when the company collapsed, they froze any stock sales, forcing victims like Roy to stand by helplessly watching the stock price and their fortunes crash right before their eyes, unable to do anything to stop it. Yet despite all that, he took it in relative stride.

"I worked all those years, sixty hours a week, so that I could retire with the fruits of my labor, and now it was all gone," said Roy. *"Now I was looking at maybe sixty-two if not seventy before I could stop working. But when you look at all those people that lost so much in 9/11, all the heartache that brought, this really pales in comparison. I still had my wife, my children, and so many people that came forward to help and voice their support. I really had a lot to be thankful for."*

Thankful, after losing everything? Where was the anger? Was this just gentle lip-service? Roy had been working since the time he was sixteen, loading beans onto a boxcar for low wages. He appeared to live a good and respectful life. He married the woman he loved, and then he spent his life taking care of her. He raised a family and responsibly supported them. He lived a temperate life, paying for the things his family needed and saving the rest so that he and his wife could retire happy and healthy one day. So why on earth was he not angrier than he was?

"I want justice done and for them to receive their fair punishment," explained Roy. *"But I don't wish them ill because that kind of bitterness can take over your life. I've never been a bitter person, and I'm not going to become one now. They hurt me as much as they could financially, but I won't allow them to hurt me emotionally too. I won't let them take anything else away from me. Besides they'll never be able to take what's really important."*

Roy said that these people did not wake up one day with the ability to deal with this loss; it resulted from a lifetime of thoughtfulness. Though it seemed as if they lost all that they had worked their entire lives for, their loss actually changed their perspective and awareness. They still had the love and respect of their families, friends, colleagues, and members of their community. Roy realized that the first week he was back on the job after the Enron implosion. *"All my customers, even the ones I didn't even know that well, offered their support,"* recalled Roy. *"The sympathy and condolences were amazing. In fact, some of these people were madder than I was about what happened to me. I had to calm them down. That really helped me to get through the first few months."*

Roy eventually spearheaded a major class-action lawsuit against Enron to try to get a small piece of the money back, inspired by the many others who were damaged. *"As much as I lost, I wasn't even the biggest loser out there,"* explained Roy. *"At least I still had my job. When you see the looks of pain and suffering on some of these people's faces—the ones who lost so much more than I did, it just breaks your heart. Sometimes, it makes me feel like I don't even deserve to feel bad at all. But I knew something had to be done to help all those people get a little bit of compensation and peace of mind."*

Charles Prestwood was one of those other victims in particular who lost much more than Roy—a total loss of $1,310,507. Even worse, he was already a few months into his retirement when the company went bankrupt. The former pipeline worker was sixty-two years old and had devoted over thirty-three years of his life to the company when he finally decided it was time to take care of his many medical conditions and to enjoy his retirement. It sounded like a great idea until his life was turned upside-down a few months later. *"I was going to do some traveling with my girlfriend,'* explained Charles. *"I had a lot of plans and dreams. I thought I had all my ducks in a row. I had enough money so I didn't have to worry about anything. But my lifestyle changed 180 degrees when that word came down about Enron."*

Instead of having a sizeable nest egg, Roy now had to get by on a $1,300 monthly Social Security check plus a $729 monthly pension. With his heart condition and progressively worsening arthritis, his health insurance costs alone ate up more than half of that. *"I've cut back on everything,"* said Charles. *"I lived my whole life right here in Texas, and did nothing but work. One day I planned to see the world. Now I don't even drive the twenty miles into town unless I have errands to run because I need to conserve on gas."*

Even though Charles was so incredibly wronged and was clearly a little more upset about it than Roy, he still saw the upside of the whole situation. *"When you lose everything, you realize the Lord is still there more than ever,"* explained Charles. *"He may not always give us what we want, but he gives us what we need. He brought my girlfriend into my life. This would be unbearable if I didn't have her, and not a day goes by now that I don't appreciate her."*

Despite the health challenges that travel poses for him because of his heart condition, he has twice made the trip to Washington DC to testify in front of the U.S. Senate because he knows there's a lot more at stake here than money. *"When you look back and see thirty-three years of your life made void by the actions of a handful of people at the top, it really hurts,"* said Charles. *"But you'll never see another Enron again because all those federal agencies that were sleeping finally woke up because of this. Now they know they got to keep an eye on these things. If I can help it from ever happening again, then at least that's something good out of all this."*

He was just as concerned about the reasons he lost it, about righting wrong and reestablishing some sense of justice in the world, which the loss will make possible. *"There's a lack of morality in the workplace nowadays,"* said Charles. *"And people don't take pride in their work. That's got to change, and it will."*

It was clearly apparent with both these men that this love and appreciation of others actually was having the very practical effect of helping them overcome their monetary loss. Now, a cynic could say their situation offered them no other choice. On the other hand, these men are faring incredibly well, given what they experienced.

Riches to Rags to Riches

Alfredo Molina is a wealthy, successful, and respected jeweler. The handsome and dapper gentleman is usually exquisitely clad in expensive pin-striped suits and designer dress shirts, capped off by bejeweled cufflinks. He has enough money to make most people's dreams come true a few times over. Yet his biggest dream is to give all his money away. *"I want to die broke,"* revealed Molina. *"I remember when my family had nothing. Now I want to make what I have possible for others."*

To that end, Molina gives away millions of dollars each year, about 60 percent of his earnings. Yet his attitude about money, making it or giving it away, was inspired by losing lots of it—twice!

From Spanish gentry roots, the Molina family did well for themselves in Cuba. Alfredo's grandfather was a master jeweler and a contemporary of Harry Winston. They owned hotels, had servants, and wanted for naught—that is, until Fidel Castro overthrew the government on New Year's Eve in 1958.

Alfredo was born into that confusion and struggle. His family lost everything overnight. They fled to America in 1967 with only one smuggled peso to their name. Upon arriving in the United States, they were fortunate enough to be accepted in Chicago as Catholic refugees. Alfredo, then only seven, still remembers vividly how tough those first days in America were. *"The hotel where we stayed was so rundown it was condemned the following year,"* remembered Alfredo. *"The place was filled with rats and the furniture was so old and worn, a puff of smoke would come up when you sat down."*

With no food on the table, Alfredo's father scrambled to find whatever work he could to support his family. However, a random act of kindness gave Alfredo his first taste of caring in a capitalist society when a perfect stranger his father met in the lobby of the hotel reached out to help. *"He took us to the grocery store and bought us a week's supply of food,"* remembered Alfredo. *"It was the first time I ever saw that much food on a shelf in my entire life."*

The stranger's generosity gave the family a jump-start. Alfredo's father lifted them out of poverty by working two jobs, one as a pipe cutter and the other as a janitor. He toiled from seven in the morning until eleven at night. They were on their way.

In the meantime, Alfredo's grandfather, who went back to work as a jeweler in America, took him under his wing to teach him the jewelry business. Every day after school, Alfredo worked on a bench under his grandfather's watchful and demanding eye, practicing on pennies rather than risking any precious metals, and honing the skill that would eventually make his dreams in America come true.

Alfredo eventually married and started his own family. He went out on his own to forge his way as a successful businessman and a jeweler. Things went well at first. Then when a partnership failed, it left Alfredo in a difficult situation. At twenty-eight, with a wife and three little mouths to feed, Alfredo lost everything again, and he was $120,000 in debt. *"I was so low,"* recalled Alfredo. *"There was no way to go but up."*

He began a new jewelry business in Phoenix in 1987. He quickly grew his business's fame by giving back many of his profits through local charities. Within ten years, Alfredo skyrocketed to success. Today he is one of the world's top gemologists specializing in supergems, which are rare, extremely high-quality and high-priced stones, and in forensic gemology. His client list now includes some of Hollywood's biggest stars and political "movers and shakers" from senators to presidents. It is a long way from the squalor of his youth, and it is also a long way from where he wants to go. *"There are a lot of wealthy people in this world who are very miserable because all they concentrate on is their money,"* said Alfredo. *"They don't understand that true wealth is what the money does and how it can give other people the hope and willingness to survive."*

Alfredo serves on seventeen different boards of charities, supports 167 different charities, and assists those he especially is concerned about—children. From Childhelp USA to the Boys and Girls Clubs of America, he constantly strives to give back what was given to him and his family. *"I believe I was put here on this earth to do great things,"* said Molina. *"But I don't think that was to do great things for me but for others. Charity has given my life meaning. My business plan is about making more so I can give more away."*

When All Is Lost

Ultimately it is possible and preferable to see money simply as a tool that allows us to take care of ourselves and those we have a duty to care for. The nature of that duty and what you are willing to do in order to serve it are far more important than the money itself. If you lose it all, it most certainly is a catastrophe because you may not be able to fend for your family and those you love. But such a situation can also make you more aware of those responsibilities and the people you love who look to you for support. It brings you that much closer to them, and if those relationships are solid, it may inspire some pretty heroic activity. Losing that money, or the ability to serve it, can be the catalyst for greater triumphs and nobler behavior than you ever thought you were even capable of doing.

Hai and his family are a good example. In Vietnam, Hai struggled for years to successfully overcome the poverty of his youth, imposed mostly by the oppression of the occupying French forces that confiscated all his family's land and unjustly executed his wife's father. By the time he had a family of five children, Hai had overcome that great adversity to obtain a relatively high standard of living. The family had a big house, a maid, all the modern conveniences of the day, a car, and a boat. Hai was a partner in a successful contracting company with an American friend he met while working in construction for the American government. One of the company's lucrative contracts was for the American Embassy, which is how he learned, weeks before the fall of Saigon, that the city was about to be overrun by Communist forces. He used his contacts and charm to secure arrangements for safe passage out of the country for his family, as well as thirty of his employees and their families.

Then everything fell apart. First, the Chase Manhattan Bank shut down with all of Hai's money in it, leaving him with $100 to his name. Then, as Hai and his staff and all their families gathered at the airport with luggage in hand to board a TWA jetliner, the Communists shelled the airport. *"The plane was about to land,"* said Hai. *"Then the bombs started and we all watched it fly away."* Hai scrambled the next day to get his family and the families of all his employees on military helicopters as the chaotic city went up in flames.

After weeks at sea on an aircraft carrier, they waited for a month in cramped quarters at a refugee camp on Wake Island. Five of the families he helped to escape refused to leave his side, still thinking that he was their superior who could take care of them. Hai realized there was very little he could do for them now, and he feared that their allegiance would inhibit their ability to succeed independently in America. So he took the $100 he had and split it among them. *"I told them, 'I am no longer your boss,'"* explained Hai. *"'Now we are all equally broke,' I said. I wanted to help them and give them hope, but I also wanted to make them independent. That would help all of us."*

Hai and his family arrived in this country with nothing more than the few dollars he kept. Their first home was a tent at Camp Pendleton, California, where they waited for several months for the right to enter the United States. Good news came when Hai was invited to come to Arizona by his old American business partner, who also made it safely out and now lived with his family outside of Phoenix.

Hai immediately enrolled in a technical school and started digging ditches and laying pipes for a contracting company with his friend. He took another job at night as a security guard. Meanwhile his wife went to work cleaning restaurants before sunrise each morning, so that she could be home in time to wake the five children for school, prepare their meals, and tend to all the housework. Hai also did his best to help her at the restaurant job after he salvaged a few hours sleep. *"She was so sad. She would cry so hard sometimes because of how difficult our lives had become,"* recalled Hai. *"I felt badly for her because she was never prepared to go out into the world and work like that. But she adjusted quickly and was very strong. We both did."*

Hai took whatever work was offered to him as he struggled to regain security for his family, and he was grateful for whatever opportunity arose. *"It's funny but we never even asked how much the job paid,"* recalled Hai. *"If it was paying work, we did it and we were grateful for the chance to take care of our family."*

People from the local community also offered help. However, Hai refused over and over again to accept charity. *"I would not take money for something I did not earn,"* declared Hai. *"I didn't want welfare or food stamps because I refused to be a burden on America. I wanted to give not take. America gave me a home. I wanted my family to make its own way to pay for that. I wanted to show my appreciation to this country."* In fact, he even convinced other Vietnamese refugees not to accept any assistance either, other than small offerings from friends. *"People were very thoughtful and they would give my wife and the other women clothes and take them shopping,"* said Hai. *"That was all right. But I would not take money. I refused."*

Even when the apartment his family was living in burned down along with everything in it a few months after they moved in, Hai refused to accept money offered by the Red Cross. *"Still I believe that is wrong,"* proclaimed Hai. *"It ruins you and makes you dependent instead of independent."*

In the end with a lot of hard work and a never-say-die attitude, Hai succeeded in moving the family out of poverty into a secure and comfortable middle-class life. His parents sent his five children to private Catholic school. Then he sent all five to college. Many of them even secured college recommendations from the honorable Sandra Day O'Conner, an Arizona native, and they all went on to great individual success as lawyers, engineers, accountants, and so on.

Hai rose up to a position of prominence with Intel in facilities management. As his position improved, he gave back first by helping many fellow Vietnamese immigrants and then by coordinating efforts to raise money for the overall local community through his company. That resulted in one of the high points of Hai's life when he represented Intel carrying the Olympic torch through the streets of Phoenix in 2002, a reward for his extraordinary efforts.

Most of his family is presently secure. Yet, they all consider primarily what they can do with their money for their family and their friends far more meaningful than having it.

"The End of the World"

America once seemed like a fantasy world, a utopia unlike any ever dreamed of in human history. Watching the evening news, reports now abound with some disaster or hardship, especially many that have occurred between 2001 and 2005 and have placed the nation in economic turmoil.

In four years, this nation was shaken by the terrorist attacks of 9/11, monumental economic breakdowns as fraudulent financiers cost employees and investors billions, wars in Afghanistan and Iraq, terrorism, and partisan rhetoric.

Hurricane Katrina practically wiped New Orleans off the map. The horrific breakdown of levees, of emergency response, and of civilization in general sent many to their deaths and many more into total desperation. Individuals responded by donating record amounts of money to help those imperiled by the storm. Foundations called the response to Hurricane Katrina stunning. Within just a few months after the disaster, the tallies showed corporate giving reaching almost $400 million and counting. Meanwhile, the individual public response to the hurricane devastation on the Gulf Coast was verging on the biggest charitable outpouring in U.S. history. Private donations reached nearly $2.7 billion by the end of 2005, according to the Red Cross and Indiana University's Center on Philanthropy. Apparently the harder things were financially, the stronger we grew as a nation and the more we wanted to give. The more we lost, the more we had to give.

So many people lost everything in Hurricane Katrina. There were many stories that showed the transition from what seemed like the end of the world to the beginning of a new and better life. *"I lost everything I had,"* revealed Ernestine McCathen to a crowded congregation of supporters gathered to raise money, support, and prayers for the victims, *"but God has something better for me, I'm quite sure."*[3] Donations at the event reached almost half a million dollars. Another family who lost everything was living under a bridge in Louisiana until they were rescued. Four months later, thanks to some very caring folks in Pennsylvania, they were living in a new house in that state, with new clothes, furniture, and money for food—all courtesy of a local community-action group that wanted to help. *"It's like waking up to a wonderland every day,"* said Shannon Graham of the amazing outpouring of kindness her family received. *"It's so amazing. It's just so beautiful."*[4]

Young author Blake Bailey lived through four different hurricanes in one year, culminating in the loss of all that his family had in New Orleans. Good friends were there to help, and fortunately they got out before the hurricane hit, taking refuge in Oxford, Mississippi. There he was overcome by the outpouring of love and support from friends and family, some of whom he had not even heard from in years, who all wanted to help. *"Mornings are bad, to be sure: that first minute after you wake up, and you remember all over again that you're broke and everything is gone and your poor old cat is dead,"* wrote Bailey. *"But there, too, is your wife's warm haunch, right where you left it, and there's the gaping baby between you."*[5]

When the end of the world comes, or we think it has because we have lost all our worldly gain, it can inspire us to realize that all the material possessions and the money it takes to buy them is just a little piece of the puzzle. However, the picture it represents is still intact in our hearts.

What Do We Need?

What do we want? What do we need? What is the difference, and does confusing the two sometimes make us overlook the very things in life we *really* want and inherently need in our souls, in our society, and in our world? Do modern society's messages convince us to be unhappy because of it?

Music videos, movies, and celebrities do their best to convince us that there is luxury, opulence, and pleasure out there that we could have, that we should want to have, that we need. Maybe we would all feel a lot better and resolve a lot more of the world's problems if we reject that type of thinking, just a little bit, exchanging it for a healthy dose of altruism and contentment. Perhaps, we just need to remind ourselves that what we need is actually not always what we want and that we do not need to have what we want.

If you want more than you could ever hope to accumulate, there is a priceless view of the world that you are offered by Christ. It is one that all the money in the world could never obtain. It is one that can never be taken from you, even if you lose all the money in the world, because you realize that the most important thing in life is the love and dignity that lives safely and securely inside the priceless human heart.

8
Let It Be
Family Troubles

A few years back, religious writer Mark Pinsky wrote a book called *The Gospel According to the Simpsons* in which he asserted that the infamous dysfunctional cartoon family, despite all its failings, was actually a deeply virtuous and loving family, and one that was ultimately very moral and appealing. Despite objections to the hit show by some fundamentalist groups, most of the country seems to agree, as families from coast to coast have embraced the adorably underachieving Homer and his irresistibly imperfect family for over two decades. Maybe that is because, even though Homer and his brood frequently say and do all the wrong things, they inevitably realize the errors of their ways and try to do better. The ultimate catalyst for that realization is their love and devotion to each other and their utter loyalty to the family unit.

Is that not how so many American families operate—loyally and imperfectly—and why we are so attracted to the Simpsons. Or why people cozied up to the Osbournes, a show about the true-life adventures of a family led by a discombobulated, recovering drug-and-alcohol addicted, former rock star, father of two punked-out adolescents who were kept in step by an unconventional but dutiful wife and mother. Even the terribly misguided criminal activities of the Sopranos, with its crime-boss dad, opportunistic mother, and juvenile-delinquent children, are somehow both horrifying yet identifiable to us.

All these families are perpetually flawed, in both trivial ways and serious, yet they also attract and interest us. Why? First of all, they hit home, literally, in the nervous identifications that we have with them. They go beyond the "characters" in their families to play up the many various flaws that all of us at one time or another find in our own families. At the end of the day, they are the stories of families that are trying to stay together yet are coming apart at the seams.

These stories appeal because they draw upon all *our* stories of *our* families: imperfect, troubled, constantly struggling to overcome the personal trials and tribulations incurred by the personal demons of parents, sibling rivalry, and the general condition of humanity on people genetically brought together to love and support each other.

What's Normal?

People are as different from each other as they can possibly be. Diverse faiths, races, socioeconomic status, and geographical places—people all have one thing in common. Each has some kind of family crisis or turmoil that in some way affects the overall outcome of their life.

A glance at history provides countless such examples. Wolfgang Amadeus Mozart, probably the most famous musical composer of all time, had an ambitious, overbearing, and disapproving taskmaster of a father, who drilled music into him and his sister from infancy. The ultimate stage father, he was a perfectionist who saw innate abilities in his children and would accept nothing less than greatness from them because of it, dragging them all over Europe to showcase their talents. The grueling schedule of touring and repeatedly practicing endangered young Wolfgang's health. His father refused to let that thwart his plans for their success and applied quick fixes to get the child up and running again in time for the next gig. Such abuse and tension severely affected Mozart in his adulthood. He struggled with emotional and physical ills until his untimely death. He walked a fine line between extreme love and adoration of his father and utter hatred and rejection of him. Ultimately all that chaos and consternation inspired extraordinary beauty in his music, which he in turn shared with the world.

Abraham Lincoln is commonly viewed by many as the greatest U.S. president ever, but the man who saved the nation from division and chaos suffered an extremely troubled family and a difficult youth. He endured the death of his brother and his mother before he was ten years old and was physically and emotionally abused by his father afterward. Lincoln was prone to depression and self-doubt because of those hardships. Perhaps that is why he despised the physical abuse of slavery and human bondage and ultimately ended it in America. Or why he fought for unity and rejected partisanship. It is ironic too that this man plagued by a childhood crisis would resolve the greatest crisis the nation has ever known, quite possibly because he had so much experience with it.

Scores of high-profile entertainers and politicians all came from troubled or broken homes. People like John F. Kennedy and Bill Clinton, Frank Sinatra and John Lennon, Oprah Winfrey and Whoopi Goldberg, just to name a few, all rose to become some of the most successful and influential people of their time. This was true despite and possibly even because their troubled youths and less-than-ideal family backgrounds constantly subjected them to the stress of seeking love in a very imperfect situation. Almost assuredly, the great achievements that these people sought and realized were in some way a result of the struggles they endured and overcame with their families.

Though the trials and tribulations that we face in our families can range from extremely troubled to simply inconvenient and frustrating, the reality is that every family has experienced some kind of internal turmoil. Yet anger with our parents or siblings might actually be the catalyst for why we strive, why we struggle, and why we work so gosh darn hard to make it on our own. If our families were perfect, comfortable places where all our needs were completely fulfilled, we would never leave the nest, and we would never grow up and go out into the world to search for more.

The most frustrating thing our families do might be to shatter the fantasy of our comfort and carefree life before we are ready for it, replacing it with the tension, the turmoil, and the stress of reality. We all seek the approval and respectful support of our parents and family.

So as for family foibles, who is to say what the norm is. When psychologists define the "norm" as the baseline or average experience, how are they to know what the average family experience is, when there is so much variation?

As undesirable as many events in and features of our family might be, it is the dress rehearsal for how we deal with conflict in general. Learning how to deal with frustrating and even absurd behavior in a positive way within our family can go a long way to understanding and dealing with that same behavior in strangers that we must deal with throughout our lives. After all, do you really think everybody we meet is going to act how we want?

The Worst-Case Scenario

Some family foibles come in the form of actual abuse and criminal neglect, which is the worst form of adversity anyone can experience, that which is damaging, deleterious, and unacceptable. Even in these situations there have been those who found a positive way to respond, first of all by getting themselves out of the situation they were in. Some of the people I encountered in my career who experienced the worst of abuses showed some of the greatest capability to forgive and reconcile; that allowed them to move on in amazing ways. They are still traumatized to a certain unavoidable degree, but the effects of that damage are far less obstructive and sometimes even constructive, versus the case of those who do not move on and let go of the pain and anger.

Olivia was one of those very amazing people who actually found a way to use the trauma of her upbringing to fuel her success and her self-esteem. Smart and successful, and possessing a razor-sharp mind and enough get-up-and-go to leave the competition in the dust, the successful thirty-year-old sales rep made her own way since she was sixteen. That is when she left home a week after being treated in the hospital for a "nasty fall" that left her with two broken ribs, a fractured tibia, and a broken nose. The fall actually occurred after her drunken mother beat the living daylights out of her for not cleaning up her room.

To hear Olivia's mother explain her reasoning at the time, she did the best she could to keep it together after Olivia's father gambled away a million-dollar ranch, including their house, in backroom poker games over the course of their twenty-year marriage. Each time her husband came home broke, it meant they were not going to pay the bills that month unless her mother brought home a little extra from her job waiting on tables. Olivia knew that as soon as her mother got home from a tough shift slinging hash, she would vent her anger by slinging punches at Olivia. It had become a tradition.

Olivia wandered through her share of hardships on the way to where she is today. At first, she pretended her parents no longer existed. She relocated to the big city lights of Las Vegas, where she got a job assisting at a real estate company while she studied for her GED. She rightly realized that she needed to distance herself physically from her abusive mother and derelict father for the time being; yet her disavowal of their existence only helped to cement the damage. She quickly got herself on her feet professionally. After going through a series of ill-fated relationships with a cavalcade of men ranging from abusive addicts to totally dispassionate father-figures, she realized that her parents and her upbringing were something she not only needed to recognize but something from which she could actually benefit. *"As soon as I stopped hating myself, I stopped hating them,"* explained Olivia. *"Their abuse gave me two choices, either give in to depression and despair, believing I was unlovable or realize the reason their abuse hurt so much was because I was healthy. The pain was the proof that they didn't destroy me."*

As soon as she felt she had been away long enough to heal physically and emotionally, she pursued a relationship again with both her parents as an adult. *"I wasn't looking for them to be my parents,"* explained Olivia. *"But it was important that I explain to them what they had done, and tried to help them to move on to a place where they could acknowledge that and heal too by becoming better people in general. Giving them the opportunity to see the error of their ways and ask for my forgiveness was as important to my growth as it was to theirs. It was another way of proving to myself that they didn't ruin me. I was still able to feel and to help them heal."*

That is exactly what she did and eventually her healthy efforts helped her father kick his gambling habit. He even put aside money to leave her when he died, only a few years after she reinitiated contact with him. It was not much, and it hardly came close to what he deprived her of in her childhood, both monetarily and figuratively. Also, her father a left her something even more valuable: his experience and sorrow.

"The last time I saw him before he died, he cried his eyes out telling me how sorry he was that he couldn't do any more for me," revealed Olivia. *"Gambling destroyed him. Seeing him like that, filled with all that regret, I realized that any money I squander on anything foolish is money that could go to a child of mine instead. I have not even bought a lottery ticket since the day he died because of it."*

For Olivia, what was even more profound was the realization on his part and hers that she *had* a father—and one who could still teach her something about life through his own loss. *"Being a part of his recovery and watching him want to get better, to want to try to make a difference in my life, meant the world to me,"* said Olivia. *"I don't ever want to be in the horrible place that he must have felt like he was in most of his life. But accepting his faults and his humanity went a long way to helping me accept mine. It made me realize that all of us are capable of being very loving and very unloving, and I want to use as much of my energy to be loving."*

Olivia's mother on the other hand was a completely different story and one that would truly test Olivia's resolve. Her mother's alcoholism escalated to a drug addiction. From cocaine to heroin, she was in and out of hospitals and rehab, and it was usually Olivia who checked her in.

Olivia has been very deliberate and careful never to let her mother overstep the boundary of respect that she has established in their relationship. *"If I can develop the ability to confront her psy-*

chosis and anger with healthy love, then it empowers me," explained Olivia. *"I come away from every encounter feeling stronger and more resolved that I'm OK. Psychologists tell me I need to be very careful if I have kids that I don't fall into an abusive pattern with them. Conquering my hatred of my mother is the best way to do that. It takes away any power she ever had over me. If I can be loving to my mother, I can love anyone."*

Though Olivia does not recommend such an ordeal to anyone, she could not deny that her ability to fend for herself has a great deal to do with having such a difficult childhood. She felt she handled it as well as could be expected. *"Once the cards are drawn, you either fold or play, as my dad always said,"* explained Olivia. *"I wanted to play. And I wasn't going to let either of them hurt me anymore than they already had. I wasn't going to let them make me into a monster. Every time I help my mom and I see the ugliness inside of her, it helps me avoid that even more."*

Olivia could not deny who she was and where she came from but she could use the lack of love in her life and the resultant pain as an inspiration to find love in her own heart. The very pain and suffering that she experienced first as a victim with her family, then as an observer and compassionate caretaker with her father and her mother, galvanized in her what she wanted and did not want in her life. Accepting the fact that she deserved their love and respect but might never get it expedited her maturity into an autonomous adult who realized that we can ask for and hope for certain behaviors from others, but we cannot force them to deliver. When they do not, it is not a reflection on our own inferiority or inadequacy but simply a confirmation of their own. We then do what we need to assure a respectful environment for ourselves to love and live in, while learning a valuable lesson about what kind of life we want to lead and what kind of person we do not want to be. No matter how much we try to avoid it, we are inexorably connected spiritually and psychologically to our parents, so we need to find a way to understand and assimilate them and our experiences with them into our lives.

A few years ago the *Oprah Winfrey* show aired a special on child abuse in which she assured abuse victims they did not have to continue to be abused and that there was help available for them and a way out of their misery.

Watching the show that day was fifteen-year-old Jennifer who, along with her younger sister, had been sexually and emotionally abused by her father since her mother died when Jennifer was only seven years old. Their father forced young Jennifer to take her mother's place cooking, cleaning, and providing sexually for the father. To keep a hold on the girls, he prohibited them from ever leaving the house without him, even keeping them from attending school. Their father's physical and emotional power over the two of them was so strong that they never fled until Jennifer saw the *Oprah* episode and finally mustered the courage to run away to a nearby police station. After they rescued her sister, they quickly put the two of them into protective custody. Her father was then arrested, prosecuted, and imprisoned.

Beyond the horrific nature of her experiences, the most astounding thing about this woman's story was that, when I interviewed her and asked her what she thought of her father, she very calmly told me that he was a disturbed and evil man who needed to be in prison. She did not hate him nor did she try to forget the experience. *"I want to remember everything that happened to me,"* she told me. *"And I want to understand him and everything about the way he thought, so that I can avoid ever getting into a relationship with anyone who has those tendencies, so I can protect my children from the same thing I experienced."* She mentioned more than a few men whom she was able to warn friends of the abusive tendencies that she spotted. More important, she felt that the lessons of survival that she learned during those years of abuse made everyday life a breeze, comparatively speaking. *"I certainly wouldn't wish this on my worst enemy,"* explained Jennifer. *"But it happened to me, and I'm still here to talk about it. My sister is safe, I have my own business, and I have achieved a successful life at a young age. I know making it through what I did had something to do with my ability to do that and enabled me to handle whatever life throws my way."*

Situations like the ones Olivia and Jennifer experienced are the worst-case scenario. However, the reality is that they exist, and those that come from such households do not have the choice of a "do over," so they are forced out of sheer survival to adopt the perspective that this whole book is about.

The Perfect Family?

One of the primary sources of anger and frustration over our family problems is the mistaken assumption that there is "a perfect family" out there, and ours always falls so short of that unrealistic image.

The experience of the Ginglen brothers illustrates this understanding. Their upstanding sixty-four-year-old father went on a crime spree robbing small-town banks in Illinois and using the money allegedly to support illicit extramarital affairs, prostitutes, and a crack habit. When the brothers saw their father in surveillance photos using a gun for the heists, they decided to turn him in, for his own protection and the protection of anyone else that he might hurt. Their father was sentenced to forty years in prison for his actions, and he wasn't very happy with his children for turning him in.

"He was out robbing banks with a gun that my brother had given him, as a gift of all things, and we needed to put a stop to it," middle son Clay, a music teacher, explained to me. *"He could have hurt a lot of people, including himself. We didn't know he was capable of doing this, so we didn't know what else he could have done."*

The father was a former Marine, who convinced his children to follow in his military footsteps, after which they all went into some form of public service, the youngest becoming a police officer and the other two serving as volunteer firemen. *"He was a very proud man who taught us to be proud,"* said Clay. *"He seemed like he had everything so under control, so we all felt like we needed to do the same. And for the most part we did because of him."* The proud father always paid his bills, took care of the family, and never seemed to have any problems, or at least any that he would show.

However, his perfect world started unraveling when he lost his job at a manufacturing company. When he could not find new work, the perfect father created the perfect secret-life, rather than admit to anyone how tough things really were. *"He was driving a brand new Cadillac even when he was out of a job,"* recalled Clay. *"I guess he was just too proud to show that he was in trouble. So he lied."*

He told his wife and family he got a job collecting receipts from vending machines in bars across the state. Then he disappeared for days at a time supposedly working. His journal, found after his arrest, showed the truth. He was robbing banks by day and was intimately involved with wanton women and buying drugs by night.

All three children were obviously devastated by what their father did and they suffered the consequences of his actions. Besides the pain and anguish he caused their mother, she was thrust into financial ruin by her husband's irresponsible actions. According to Clay, the boys' mother was held responsible for restitution of thousands of dollars of debt, which her husband ran up to support his double life.

Even though all three sons were subjected to the same situation and took the same action, the reasons for their actions and the ways they reacted internally were completely different. The youngest son, Jared, a police officer who first saw the incriminating photos of his father and alerted the other brothers, was so incensed that he refused to speak to his father. Garrett, the eldest brother, whose gun was used in the robberies, was equally upset. According to Clay, he felt pressured to fix the whole situation, but did not know how.

Clay quickly forgave his father. He was able to simultaneously understand that his father had done a terrible thing, yet without carrying great resentment or anger in his heart toward him. Clay was able to move past the pain and anger to evaluate the situation rationally without feeling irreparably damaged by it. *"I know he was not purposely trying to hurt us with his actions,"* he said. *"He must have some type of personality disorder that made it possible for him to lie this much and pull this off. That doesn't excuse his actions at all, but I can see his side. My mom always taught us to be forgiving, and I took that to heart. Now I just want to try to help Mom however way I can."*

Why Clay believes his other brothers dealt so differently with their father was that, maybe in some way or another, they felt that their father's actions were a reflection on them. In fact, Jared actually commented to a reporter that he first noticed his father in the photos because he looks a lot like his father, only younger. Clay's eldest brother felt connected to his father through duty. He felt responsible for the family.

Clay used the whole situation to affirm his own autonomous values, to take the good of what his family offered, and to critique the rest in a healthy way. His father, despite his flaws, always taught the boys to do the right thing, so they did. Their mother taught them to forgive, so Clay did. Though he was obviously upset about the whole situation, he could still see the value of it, and that even helped him to explain it to his own children. *"It's a lesson for all of us,"* explained Clay. *"And that's how we're helping them to understand what happened to their grandfather."*

The Rest of Us

Of all the people I have interviewed, those who have the healthiest perspective and are the least damaged by family problems are those who realize that you cannot change your family. You must accept them with all their flaws, demanding only that they respect your rights. Factor in that we are all human, and it is somewhat implausible to believe that any family could be completely "functional."

Most of those trials and tribulations are what also lead *us* to be functional. We do not have to be imprisoned by the difficulties imposed by our parents, but we can be inspired by them. Our relationships with them can actually lead us not only to solving our issues with them, but help us to resolve many issues with others through the resilience that we learned from tolerating family troubles. After all, "You can't fire your family," said a recent seminar participant. "So what can you do to deal with the situation?" Asking yourself that question and then taking the necessary steps will develop in you a powerful resilience that will serve you in many other relationships throughout your life.

The Alternative

A tiny baby born prematurely after his mother mysteriously collapsed and died barely six months into her pregnancy left the child without something I have always had—a mother.

By some miracle and the quick and heroic acts of friends, family, and a whole lot of hard-working doctors and nurses, the 1 pound, 8 ounce child survived, delivered through Caesarian section after attempts to resuscitate his mother proved hopeless. It is truly a blessing that despite the tragedy of the mother's death, the child was saved. However, the harsh reality is that the child must now fare in the world without the comfort of his mother.

The baby's loving father was now left to parent his family alone, which also included his two-year-old daughter. He will undoubtedly learn to fill the role of mother and father, and this challenge may prove to yield even more miracles for the family as they walk down this road together.

After experiencing initial sorrow, sympathy, and hope for the family, we are reminded that those of us who have both parents and have always known the love, comfort, and support of two parents are fortunate. There are currently millions of children with no parents or family at all, either because they were born into unfortunate circumstances or because they were later removed from unhealthy circumstances. Due to the "big hearts of many" across this country, according to the National Adoption Information Clearinghouse (NAIC), a service of the Children's Bureau, fortunately over 110,000 of those children are adopted each year.

Many of those domestic refugees remain essentially homeless unless they reach eighteen. Then they are cast out without the benefit of ever having had parents to raise them in the way of the harsh and cruel world. No matter how well they adapt, they will always be orphans without a family support structure. They will never know the true meaning of family.

No matter how imperfect your family may seem to you at times, if they are there and they are devoted to you, however imperfectly, then that is a whole lot more than a lot of people can lay claim to.

Sometimes in this highly interactive, very connected world of the twenty-first century, it is easy to be so overcome by the problems of the *big* world that we become overwhelmed, feeling incapable and impotent to make a difference. But it is really in the *small* world with our loved ones where we ultimately will find the answers to solving the problems of the big world, as we see the worth, importance, and possibilities of humanity in and through their eyes.

So take a moment or two to shut off the TV, overlook the morning paper, and focus on nothing but your family, and while reveling in their value, you will become reacquainted with the value of the whole of humanity. You will realize what you are working every day so hard to provide for, what we are doing on this planet in the first place, and why God created us.

9
Why Love Never Dies
Death of Loved Ones

A few decades ago, the movie *Harold and Maude* featured a character who was a rich, young man whose wealthy and unloving parents had done their best to raise him in a safe yet emotionally vacuous environment. He wanted for nothing, except to feel. He was so dead inside that he became obsessed with death, actually fantasizing about his own, hoping for an end to his miserable and meaningless existence. While entertaining one of his favorite hobbies, attending strangers' funerals, he ran into an elderly woman who also was obsessed with death but for a completely different reason. She cherished the opportunity that death brings—a new beginning. The mismatched pair winds up falling head over heels in love with each other and into a very controversial romantic relationship that is cut short when the woman discovers she is dying. While she is on her deathbed, her young sobbing suitor tells her that he will not be able to go on without her. She tells him to go out and love some more.

The pain that he was feeling at her impending death was a great demonstration of love, the love that her life was a testament to and something he was incapable of feeling before meeting her. So now it was time for her death to inspire him to go and love some more.

As simple as that sounds, it is actually the great goal and purpose of our lives and our deaths, yet one of the hardest things to remember—to help spread love and inspire those who are left behind without us to go and love some more. People who donate their bodies to science after their death essentially make it possible for them to keep loving the world by enabling others to do so more effectively.

We do not need to stop feeling the emotion that surrounds death, only we must also try to turn that sorrow into a passionate tribute to our loved one by making their life, their love, and their light a small piece of our own that we carry with us for the rest of our lives. In that way, with each passing of one soul, another soul becomes twice as bright, increasing infinitely the light of the world.

Life Is for the Living

When I was a child, I disliked going to funerals. It was not that they were frightening or depressing, or that I was uneasy around the dead, but because it meant being thrust into the midst of relatives and family friends that I did not really know. For a boy who was relatively introverted, that was a fate worse than death.

However, Italians, especially Italian mothers, are big on the whole death ritual. Every time a friend or relative died, we were usually asked to spend the night in mourning. Though I did not realize it at the time, with every passing, my mother's dramatic overtures made me appreciate and honor life all that much more. The very thing I dreaded about funerals was the best part of those experiences.

The deaths of loved ones and the celebrations of their lives that follow bring families, people, and even societies together more than just about any other single event. It does not always mean that people will be brought together harmoniously. On the contrary, some of those reunions are rife with infighting and animosity. All those human interactions are at least proof that we are alive, that we can feel, and that we do feel a sense of loss. In addition, funerals force us into contact with the community of our friends and family, even those we may not know or like much. In that way, the person who dies wakes us up to even more of our own life.

Funerals are not only about people coming together but an opportunity to absorb all the life lessons the deceased can teach us. We do our best to pay homage and respect to the dead at the funeral itself, but when the eulogist attempts to sum up a person's existence in a few words, it is usually hopelessly incomplete and inaccurately flattering. After the eulogy lies the real outpouring of emotions, stories, shared experiences, and lessons taught and learned because of the individual who has passed. These usually occur in table talk, whispers, and late-night phone calls between family and friends for weeks and months after the funeral.

For instance, my grandfather came to live with us when I was about twelve years old. He was a compulsive gambler who squandered his family's money, forcing them into poverty. Then he abandoned them to start a brand new life for himself, totally unrepentant of what he had done. Despite these actions, my father took him in when he was in his seventies, sending me a great message about forgiveness and love. My grandfather's death when I was graduating from college sent me even more of a message. There were not many people at his funeral, but those who showed up were surprising. My family and my father were of course present, as well as his daughter and her husband. Also present were some very good friends and a very elegant and special woman he loved for the last years of his life. This was a great reflection of the dichotomy of his life and a lesson on the results of life and love. My grandfather fathered children, and he chose a woman to mother those children who was such a good mother she was able to counteract his negative influence so well that these children still loved him enough to come to his funeral. He did his best to be a better man, if not ever a really good one, later on in life. I still recall my father shedding a few tears that day, even though he probably could not understand why. Whether he actually ever knew the great value I received from his actions and emotions, I don't know.

The love you take is equal to the love you make, to borrow a phrase from an old Beatles song. There are many ways to make that love and to take that love along with your opportunities to change your life and to get yet another chance to spread some love before you die. One way or another, there will be a reckoning of the meaning and relevance of your life, and it will not only be when you face your maker. It will be how your memory inspires either love and life, or sadness and death. Either way, the death of loved ones will make a difference. My grandfather's death made me realize all that, and what greater lesson could there be for a young man just embarking on his own journey.

To Live Better!

In the grand scheme of things, we cannot know why the Lord allows all the things that occur to happen, but we can open our hearts to the possibilities, the knowledge, and the lessons that the deaths of others offer.

J. D. was a young employee at a coffee shop. The fair-haired, easy-going, and physically fit seventeen-year-old always looked like he was ready to hit the beach in search of the next wave. To many, his outward appearance indicated that he did not have a care in the world. After serving me an afternoon espresso, he inquired as to what kinds of things I wrote. Just as I thought I was boring him with better ways of looking at life's tough times, he astounded me. *"Oh you mean like what happened to me this week-end?"* he said in his characteristic carefree demeanor. His cool tone totally unbefitting of anything serious or somber, I assumed he was poking fun. *"OK, what happened to you this weekend?"* I replied. *"My friend shot himself, while I was standing right next to him,"* said J. D. as if he was telling me the day's weather forecast.

Totally shocked and horrified, I stumbled into the commensurate *"I'm sorry."* Then I gingerly prodded him for the whole story. He and a few of his other friends were at a friend's apartment when one of them pulled out a shotgun and started showing off, waving it in the air, and acting like he was a real sharpshooter. *"He was laughing about it,"* revealed J. D., *"telling us it was no big deal because it wasn't loaded."* When his friend upped the ante of his antics, by pointing it at the others, J. D. had enough.

"My parents told me a hundred times never to point a gun at anyone, even if it's not loaded, and I knew that he was messed up," he explained. *"So I pushed the barrel of the gun away from us and told him to knock it off."*

That one moment, that one simple act, inspired by a few simple words he heard his parents utter many years before saved J. D.'s life and the lives of the others in the room, all except the crazed culprit. For then he turned the gun on himself and fired.

For the family of the victim, this was a great tragedy, as it was for J. D. and his friends. It will also undoubtedly remain one of those stirring experiences that in one way or another affects the rest of their lives, and they will *have* the rest of their lives to learn, to grow, and to not make the same mistakes their friend made. J. D. is already thinking more about the way he lives his life, the way he had lived it, and what is important. He has grown even closer to his parents because of it, and he is looking for more meaning in his life. He is especially thankful to his parents. For the first time in his young life he is seeing the wisdom and maturity of grownups as a good thing. For the family of the victim, they will undoubtedly have an even more difficult journey but not one without the possibility of meaning, purpose, and value.

Love After Death

Obviously, none of us wants to lose those we love, but if we accept the mysterious majesty of God and all the possibilities that suggests, then we should be open to all the possible meaning and purpose that can be found in the deaths of our loved ones. Surely if we live to love, then we should be joyous when we realize the love that the departed are able to inspire in their passing. Sometimes faith in that greater plan is the only route to a greater understanding and solace. Once you accept the Lord's plan and the death of loved ones as a part of it, it leads you to a mission and mindset. Despite this, it never gets easy to lose someone you love.

Terri Schiavo, the Florida woman whose husband wanted to end her life after she was diagnosed permanently vegetative, was allowed to starve to death by having her feeding tube removed at the request of that husband. He maintained it was her wish that her life should not be continued by any extraordinary means.

Her parents, her brother, and her sister fought fervently to prolong her life. They argued that Terri, whose eyes were open and who they claimed was still able to smile, was able to acknowledge their presence and was, in fact, alive and aware of her life. Cutting off her food supply would therefore be murder. They insisted she had always let them know that in such a situation she would want to live. *"Our family is very close,"* explained her brother Bobby Schindler to me as he talked about trying to derive meaning from her death. *"We are all very devoted Catholics and believe in the sanctity of life. To suggest that she would have suddenly changed her entire philosophy on the subject without us knowing it was ludicrous."*

The whole unfortunate ordeal began in 1990 when then twenty-six-year-old Terri collapsed at her home and her brain was deprived of oxygen for several minutes. The cause of the collapse was never medically determined, but the result was severe brain damage. Her heart and lungs functioned on their own, and she could even move her limbs, but she required a feeding tube for nourishment.

Terri continued to live that way for fifteen years. At first, her husband Michael Schiavo and Terri's family all hoped to rehabilitate her. However, in 1998, Michael Schiavo reversed his position and filed a petition to have her feeding tube removed, claiming Terri told him privately years earlier that she would not want to be kept alive by artificial means if she succumbed to an injury which required such. A seven-year battle ensued with her family who fought for her life, claiming she would never have expressed such a thought as a devout Roman Catholic who valued first and foremost the sanctity of life.

The battle rose to a national discussion as Florida's Governor Bush, the President, the Congress, and the Supreme Court all weighed in on the issue of whether or not Terri Schiavo's feeding tube should be removed. Terri's family continually argued and provided experts to argue that Terri was responsive in a variety of ways to their presence, while her husband presented experts to refute them. *"It was like an emotional boxing match,"* said Bobby. *"We couldn't understand why anyone would want to try so hard to end someone's life."*

Ultimately under Florida law, a feeding tube was considered a form of artificial life support likened to a respirator. A judge believed Michael Schiavo's allegation that Terri had expressed to him that she did not want to be kept alive by artificial means and thus ordered her tube removed. She died a little over a week later. The rift between her family and her husband culminated in his request that the police order the family out of her presence in her final hours of life as she died in a hospice.

Without passing judgment on Michael Schiavo, or anyone who believed removing the tube was the right thing to do, watching a member of your family be starved to death must rank with just about the most painful and horrible experiences possible—especially when you know preventing it is as easy as giving that person something to eat. *"It was so emotionally draining,"* recalled Bobby. *"Our faith was the only thing that gave us the strength to deal with it. That and the realization that my sister had fought so hard to hang on for so many years. She inspired us to keep going in so many ways."*

The family was obviously traumatized by the event. Yet from the moment Terri Schiavo died, they focused on the good that could come from her death; namely, hoping to inspire a national referendum on the value and supreme sanctity of life, at a time when its value is continually compromised by an ever-sophisticated society in our nation. *"There was no evidence that she ever said she wanted to die,"* said Bobby. *"And with so much contradictory information offered, it was crazy that any judge would err on the side of death. We realized that we have a culture of death in this country. If we can do something to stop others from experiencing what we had to and if we can change public policy then her death will have some meaning. All human life is sacred. Nobody has the right to take another human life."*

In a statement released to the press shortly after her death, the family expressed their hope for the future that was inspired by Terri's life and death. *"Terri, your life and legacy will continue to live on, as the nation is now awakened to the plight of thousands of voiceless people with disabilities that were previously unnoticed,"* they declared. *"Your family intends to stand up for the other 'Terri's' around this nation and we will do all that we can to change the law so others won't face the same fate that has befallen you....God's plan for Terri is unfolding before our eyes."*[1]

After a few weeks of mourning, the family began forming the Terri Schindler Schiavo Foundation (www.terrisfight.org) calling for March 31, the day she died, to be remembered as "Terri's Day," a day dedicated to the culture of life. Through the foundation the family works hard to bring attention to others like Terri who cannot speak for themselves while they lie in hospitals, nursing homes, or hospices across the nation. The family hopes to inspire people across the country to institute a series of precautions that will safeguard their own lives should they become incapacitated, yet wish to go on living. They may never get over the pain of her passing, but they are doing their best to make use of their passion for progress rather than pity. *"It's never going to make her death easier to handle,"* said Bobby. *"Even today it hits you at certain times, you can't believe that these people did what they did to her. But at least we are carrying on and doing what she would have wanted for others, so maybe we could make a difference."*

The Legacy of Life

The Schindlers could have simply given up and become so bitter over the whole experience of Terri's death that they spent the rest of their lives angry and embittered. Instead they believed there was a value in focusing on what could come of her death. They also had faith *in* their faith, accepting that God knew a little more than they did about the purpose of Terri's life and death. When we tell ourselves that God works in mysterious ways, the saying can seem to cynical observers like nothing more than an inane pleasantry, a cop-out to ease the pain or something to say when nothing else will suffice. Albert Einstein's saying about the mysterious being the greatest thing in the universe really does ring true when it comes to the mystery of life and death.

When Christ overcame death, it was so that we all could do the same through him. His death, his sacrifice, and his resurrection are what made it possible for all of us to have eternal life. In a way, every death here on earth can be a catalyst for the rebirth of someone else. The shock that surrounds the death of loved ones often makes us examine our own lives, consider whether we want to continue to live the way we have been living, or take a new path inspired by the life of the individual that was lost. The death of one can thereby change or inspire the lives of millions. This was obviously the power of the martyrdom of the saints throughout the ages.

Everyday people can similarly inspire such a legacy, even when they are surrounded by what threatens to be the death of their own spirits brought on by the death of others. A culture of life is a state of mind, as is a culture of death. As long as you are alive, you have the opportunity to pick up the torch that the departed carried and to carry it even higher and let it burn even brighter. To do that you must allow yourself to realize that somewhere out there the spark, the love, and the light of your dearly departed are burning exponentially brighter in the hearts of many others that are more alive than ever because of their life and their death.

A few years ago, a woman who worked as a financial analyst for Morgan Stanley narrowly escaped from the World Trade Center. On the morning of the 9/11 attacks, when the first plane hit the North Tower, the force of the explosion was so intense it shattered the window of her office in the South Tower, showering her with glass and sending her and colleagues running for cover. She came face to face with Rick Rescorla.

Rick was a highly decorated Vietnam war hero, whose quick-thinking, altruistic leadership saved and comforted scores of men in one of the war's first major battles in a place called the Ia Drang Valley, where American forces were on the defensive, surrounded and up against insurmountable 10 to 1 odds.

After the war, he laid down his weapon and went to work for Morgan Stanley as head of security for their Trade Center offices. His biggest concern was saving lives. For years he thought of various ways that the buildings could be attacked, and all the ways he could get people out safely in those situations.

Years before the first Trade Center bombing in 1993 he predicted the towers were vulnerable to a bomb detonated in the basement. Prior to 9/11, he told his superiors that the next time it would be a plane filled with gas.

So he prepared. He ran the employees through drill after drill until they knew how to get out of that building in their sleep. He prepared contingency plans for his contingency plans.

Then on the morning of the attacks, as the authorities instructed everyone to stay put, he led a civilized charge out the door with a bullhorn telling people to get out, no matter what anyone else said. His well-laid plans worked like clockwork.

Thanks to Rick, along with other employees of Morgan Stanley, the lives of many were saved, except Rick and a few other security personnel who helped him go back to assist those from other companies.

Interviewing Rick Rescorla's wife shortly after his death back in 2001, she was obviously traumatized by her loss. In fact, she could barely speak without sobbing between breaths. She did take great solace in the life that came out of his death. Many were grateful for Rick's diligence, preparedness, and dutiful courage but there was no way then for her to know the true ramifications of his actions.

All of us may never know about all the life that comes from the deaths of our loved ones, but if we look around us and inside our own hearts, we can get a good hint. For it is there that we are sure to find a starting point for realizing the legacy of love that will honor and memorialize our loved one, transforming our loss into the greatest and most magical of gains.

Carrying On

In Steven Spielberg's blockbuster World War II epic, *Saving Private Ryan,* a young soldier loses his three brothers in combat. This makes him a hardship case, eligible to go home at once. But he knows none of this because he's on the front lines. The Secretary of War himself dispatches a special unit of men to risk life and limb to rescue the private. In doing so, many of them are killed, including the film's star, Tom Hanks, who in his dying words orders Ryan to *"earn this."*

When death knocks at your door, you have only a couple of choices. You either hide in your house, living in desperation, anger, and fear, or you answer the door and confront it in a positive way. Whether it is continuing the good work of those that have already passed, or doing even more or better than those that departed, many are prodded to go forward and love the world in an ever-greater way, just like the young man from *Harold and Maude*.

Jany Deng, one of the famous Sudanese Lost Boys, spent most of his life surrounded by senseless and uncommonly savage deaths. Since the mid-eighties, the African nation of Sudan has been adversely affected by an almost constant civil war, as those from different ethnic backgrounds, regions, and religions battle for their right to rule over the rest. The result has been a virtual sea of bloodshed and civil unrest that seems to go on indefinitely. Amidst this chaos, tens of thousands of young boys, some as young as four years old, were orphaned by the violence. Jany Deng was one of those boys.

Tending to his family's cattle, six-year-old Jany was suddenly shaken by the thunder of exploding bombs and bullets ripping his world into scores of shattered lives. He watched in horror as his home burned to the ground, with many family members still trapped inside. *"The fire was so intense that I could feel it from the fields,"* said Jany, as he shared his compelling story with me so that others might learn from it. *"The flames were everywhere. And everyone was running and screaming. I was so young, I could not even fully comprehend what was happening until much later."* Men and boys were murdered while women and girls were raped, killed, or forced into slavery.

Running for his life, Jany and thousands of others just like him set out unguarded and alone on a treacherous, epic journey that would last over a decade in search of safety and freedom from the murderous factions that had killed their parents and wanted them dead. Named the Lost Boys by the international community that eventually came to their aid, they first headed toward Ethiopia, hundreds of miles away, walking for months in sub-Saharan heat. Many died from starvation or thirst. The weaker and younger ones were attacked and killed by wild animals. Survivors watched vultures feed on the bodies of the dead. *"I had made many friends who died along the way,"* recalled Jany. *"But there was nothing any of us could do but to keep going. When they died you stepped over their bodies and tried not to look back. It was difficult. There was so much death around us for so many years, and it never got any easier to see."*

Those that survived the first leg of their journey stayed in refugee camps for several years in Ethiopia. When the government there changed hands, the new unsympathetic regime sent soldiers to kill them. *"The helicopters came and dropped bombs on our camp all of a sudden, and many were killed,"* recalled Jany. *"It was just luck that I was not one of those that died that day."* Frantically they fled again, this time for Kenya. When they reached the crocodile-filled Gilo River at winter's high mark, they were forced to choose between awaiting the sure death promised by the soldiers behind them or taking their chances in the river. Many drowned or were eaten by crocodiles after making the only choice that made sense. For the next year, they dragged their tired, malnourished bodies on a thousand-mile trek back through Sudan and over into Kenya. With no food, they foraged on whatever they could find along the way, from bugs to bark. Once again many starved to death. *"Every day you just walked and walked,"* explains Jany. *"We ate grass and leaves—whatever we could find. We were so hungry and so afraid. Sometimes it was easy to want death to come now rather than waiting in fear for it to come in a much more painful way later."*

Jany watched many of the friends he had made along the way die horrible deaths. Only about half of the 22,000 Lost Boys eventually made it alive to Kenya in 1992, where international relief workers finally began to offer help.

In 1995, many of the Lost Boys finally made their way to the United States, a welcome relief from the horror and hardship they knew most of their lives. Jany Deng was one of those young boys. He arrived here when he was sixteen years old, along with his older brother Simon who was three years older. Jany was fortunate enough to be taken in by a caring and supportive family in Arizona. They sent him to high school and helped him acclimate to America. His brother Simon was not as fortunate and never could adjust to the diametrically different culture and life in America. One day in 1997, he walked into the Catholic Charities office in Phoenix waving a shotgun. When he refused to obey police officers' instructions to lay down his weapon, he was shot and killed.

After all Jany had been through, one might wonder what impact the death of his brother might have upon him. *"You live life and you manage to overcome so much, why?"* said Jany. *"Partly because you believe in God, and you have faith that he has a purpose for your life and for your death as well as the life and death of others. But also if he allows you to live while others die, that means you have that much more of a duty to serve him and to work hard to do more. If God helped me to survive through so much when so many others around me did not, then I was responsible to make his blessing on me worthwhile."*

Jany was determined to succeed and to carry on the legacy of his family. He also felt called to help make the world a better place, a place where other boys would never experience what he did, and where other families would never be extinguished the way that his was.

After he graduated from high school, he earned his degree in social work while working part-time at a counseling and relief center for other Lost Boys in Phoenix. He has traveled all over the nation visiting high schools to share his childhood experiences and hardships with teens in an effort to educate and inspire them to overcome their own difficulties with nobility and purpose. He hopes to work for the United Nations, and maybe even to return to his native country one day to rebuild it.

"I want to help all my brothers and sisters," said Jany. *"Because I can, because I have been given this opportunity. The experiences I had are not mine to use to feel sorry for myself, they are a gift which can help me to help others. That is why I am still here."*

Passing the Torch

It has been said that a man does not become a man until the death of his father. There is a certain figurative wisdom in this saying that suggests that the deaths of those we love sometimes breathe new life, new vigor, and new determination into those that are left behind to carry the torch. The anger, the sadness, the pain, and all the other passionate power that is called forth by the death of those we love can be some of the most tremendously inspiring and galvanizing energy that we will ever experience in our lives. It can give us courage, wisdom, direction, and purpose. It can make us do things that we never thought we would have the fortitude to do.

Coretta Scott King became a great civil-rights spokesperson because of the slaying of her husband. *America's Most Wanted* creator and star, John Walsh, became an efficacious crime-fighting advocate after the brutal, unsolved abduction and murder of his son. Obviously, those who are faithful and believe in God and an afterlife with God rejoice in the knowledge that our loved ones are going forward on their spiritual journey. Ultimately, the mystery of the afterlife makes it impossible to truly understand or appreciate fully what death will offer to those that we love.

For us survivors, what we can understand is the need to go on living better, stronger, and fuller lives in their names. We can take great pride in knowing that now it is our turn to carry on God's work here on earth for those that we loved and those whom we continue to love.

10
What's the Point?
Bad Choices, Dead Ends, and Giving Up!

Getting over the death of a loved one can be grueling and difficult, but sometimes your own metaphorical death can be even tougher. Did you ever feel like your life was over? Not because of ill health or impending physical death but because of death of the soul or the psyche. Or you are convinced you are at the end of the line because you have made as many bad decisions as you could possibly ever imagine making. Maybe you've lost your confidence, or you simply cannot pull yourself out of a seemingly difficult situation. You are ready to throw in the towel and give up.

Everyday, many people find themselves in the same situation. Their life goes from hopeful to hopeless before they even realize what happened.

Tragically, these feelings sometimes can end our life before its time when they lead to suicide or to a slow death caused by drug or alcohol abuse or other addictions before we have a chance to understand fully what is happening. That is when we must realize that, though our desperate feelings and the terrible experiences that inspire them may be real, they are only part of the picture of our lives. In fact, our feelings could be signaling the death of a part of our life, the part that is destructive or stagnant, and they could be a sign or catalyst for new life or rebirth ahead.

God designed us so that our psyches know when we are caught up in destructive or distracting behavior, or when we are just ready for a change in direction. We know it, and we feel it through that feeling of impending death inside our souls. Depression, melancholy, frustration, pain, and anger are all powerful and potent containers of energy that can be used to accomplish great things and to spur us on, when they are perceived as signposts. In the case of overriding feelings of failure and finality, we are being informed that we cannot go on living the way we were or that we are being summoned to some very positive act. Until we look at it that way, all we see is death.

The Ultimate Rise

Do you want to live forever? You can if you follow Christ's example right to the pearly gates of heaven. What we all sometimes forget is that this amazing dominion over death extends into every aspect of our existence, not just after our physical death but while we are still alive too. It summons us to be hopeful and positive proofs of his almighty power and love. It is our honor and mission to be his beacons, never dimming under the shadows of life's turmoil.

Christ rose from the dead—physically, literally—releasing us all from the grip of death, and giving us the possibility of immortal life in heaven, life that will also be literal and physical. Until then, through Christ we have the power to rise metaphorically *during* life from the mire of the temporal destruction and death that threatens to kill our souls in this world as we prepare for our eternity in the next. Jesus showed us all that through his example and faith in his father, every one of us can conquer the many forms of death that threaten to darken our lives and extinguish our light us as we live our lives in this world. Through Christ we can overcome everything and anything that comes our way.

So if we accept the Lord's love and mission, then we are no longer slaves to our weakness, our pain and suffering, our errors and sins, our experiences, and our senses, because all of those things are just parts of our journey to enlightenment.

Now, we may experience a great deal of pain and suffering along the way in life, as we set out on our path to life and love. Various biblical passages explain to us that our ultimate joy will be only experienced in heaven but that does not mean that our lives here will be filled with nothing. The life-giving power of the Lord is alive and well in this world. We can receive and experience it every day, but we must open our heads and our hearts to it.

As in the case of all the tragedies and hardships presented here, those who have not sunk to the depths of despair cannot realize the heights of joy. People who have died and been brought back to life often talk about a bright light at the end of a long tunnel. They almost unanimously have a renewed sense of purpose and joy in their lives.

Sometimes the point at which we feel completely and totally empty, void of any direction and purpose, complete and utter failures in some way, can be the most inspiring. Empirically speaking, that point can mean many different things for each of us, some more disastrous than others. When you come to that point, when the cycle of pain or suffering you experience is so extreme that it can ironically shake you out of your cycle of pain and suffering, it is like being hit over the head by a lead pipe. The impact is so intense it leaves an impression that can never be removed. It is the culmination of all the tragedies described in this book.

Regardless of the reasons why we are in that place where we *need* to be hit over the head, and regardless of how severe our failure is in our eyes or the eyes of others, it ultimately sends us down the road to realizing the seven steps of serenity described in chapter 3. We are forced by circumstance to focus on a different set of priorities than before. We are forced to view ourselves in a different way than we have ever before, and we are forced to act in a way we never thought we would or even could. We are forced to confront reality humbly, to give up a little of our own egos, and to accept the truth of a love-inspired life in the many forms that God sends it to us.

Good to the Last Drop

The Live and Let Live Café in downtown Phoenix came into existence only because the owners faced and overcame fierce drug and alcohol addictions that almost killed them. Three of the four owners are in various stages of recovery, and they decided that after overcoming their own demons and being reborn into a happier and more meaningful life, they wanted to help others do the same.

The crowd is by no means limited to the owners' recovering peers; many simply come for the coffee and the food. You can hear one of the owners or another patron inspiring or uplifting someone whose light is not so bright right now. Whether suffering addiction or the weight of the world heavy upon your shoulders, the café is a great and inspiring place where anyone can let their cup runneth over in a relatively healthy way.

One of the patrons said to another, *"The void in your life can inspire you to fill it with something healthy and positive like helping others."* The fact that they were at the end of their rope is what inspired the owners to kick their addictions and eventually led them to creating this café and sharing their triumphant story.

"I know that if I even have one drink that things will go back to exactly the way they were when I had that last drink," said Doug, one of the owners, who has been in recovery for over a decade. *"I have so many friends and family members that I value, and I would lose all that."*

From a typical middle-class family in Arizona, Doug started drinking when he was a teenager, like a lot of youths, to get over his shyness. *"I did it to break the ice,"* said Doug. *"It gave me something I thought I was missing in my life and in my personality."*

By the time he got to college, he was drinking every day and could not even think of starting the day without a drink. *"I took beer to class with me,"* admitted Doug. *"I thought everybody did."* In his junior year, he passed out during an exam. Not long after that Doug failed out of school.

His drinking problem was only the beginning of his personal problems. He became hooked on crack cocaine, feeding a quarter-ounce-a-day habit. He knew he was in trouble but had no clue how to get himself out of that place, even if there was a way out.

Years later Doug realized that his drug addiction was actually one of the best things that ever happened to him. *"I would have gone on in secret as a functional alcoholic for years without ever getting help, and it would have probably killed me eventually,"* explained Doug. *"My parents knew I was drinking, but they didn't understand how bad I was. Once they found out about the drugs they put me into rehab immediately."*

After fourteen days in rehab and six months in outpatient group therapy, he replaced the need for drink and drugs with the desire to reach out to others, first to his family and friends, and then to other users in the group. He eventually went back to school and earned his bachelor's degree, and then went on to earn his MBA and become a manager for a major national restaurant chain. He has been clean and sober ever since.

At a meeting for recovering addicts he met Gail. Like him, she sank so low, she had nowhere to go but up, and she was tired of hurting herself and the people she loved.

By the time she was twelve, the daughter of well-to-do Seattle suburbanites was nursing a half-gallon-of-gin habit. *"I mixed it with raspberry Kool-Aid,"* said Gail. *"I always saw adults making mixed drinks, so I figured it was a good idea. I hated the taste of it, but I plugged my nose and I drank it anyway. That's how you know you're an alcoholic, when you hate drinking, but you do it anyway."*

Despite her alcoholism, Gail grew up to hold down a good job in the corporate security business and make a successful life for herself financially. Like Doug, one addiction soon led to another. Soon she was trying it all. She would get hooked and then quit. In 1989, her world came crashing down when she started dating a heroin addict. *"I told myself that if I got hooked on heroin and then quit, I could help him do it too,"* explained Gail. *"Well there's a whole lot of movies from 1989 until 1994 that are completely new to me because I was completely gone during that time."*

The addiction robbed her of everything she had, and in just a few years, she disintegrated to a sickly 98-pound heroin junkie living by herself underneath a bridge with three-fourths of her lungs overcome by pneumonia. One day she called her mother and begged her for help.

"I knew I was finally done when I made that phone call," said Gail. *"She immediately got me into a treatment center."*

Since her own rehabilitation, Gail has helped over 150 people work through their own recovery. What she learned through all of it was that for many of us in today's world, our own egocentrism, pride, and selfishness actually stand in the way of us ever really growing up and finding our purpose in the world. Once you are forced by circumstance to give up all that, then you find the life that makes you want to keep living.

"No matter how you say it, the truth is that there is something greater than yourself," explained Gail. *"Only someone who has lost everything can tell you with any degree of certainty that they know material things don't matter—that they are just a part of all that's really out there in life. And only when you realize you aren't at the center of the universe do you find what is. I have seen so many amazing recoveries happen over the years that made people realize that."*

Today neither Doug nor Gail make excuses for their past behavior and former addictions. They tell no hard-luck tales other than the ones of their own making. They both know how it feels to be in a difficult situation from which there seems to be no way out. They realized the answer was right in front of them in the pain and suffering they felt, and how they could use it to inspire them to step away from themselves so they could understand, identify, and help others. They opened the café on Valentine's Day in 2005, as if to be the ultimate gift of love to everyone in the neighborhood. *"We wanted to make a comfortable place for anybody coming in off the street to get a little relief,"* said Doug. *"Seeing people smile and to see all our hard work appreciated and making a difference in people's lives is what makes life and this place all worth it. And it's a much healthier way to overcome my shyness."*

True Freedom

Certainly, like Doug and Gail, none of us can go on living our lives lost in our own world of illusory pleasure, pain, or confusing combination of both. When that world is as destructive as theirs was, we are made that much more aware of it by our failure. When our egocentrism is experienced in subtler and less destructive ways, it may take longer to realize it. In the popular U.S. culture where it seems that egocentric and duplicitous behavior is tolerated and often greatly rewarded in the short term, it can take much longer to realize its damage. Sooner or later, destructive behavior leads you to realization. Sometimes our own egos take us there whether we consciously want it or not, and the truth shall set us all free—eventually.

In 2006 a scandal erupted over the best-selling book *A Million Little Pieces* by author James Frey. The book, which Frey claimed to be an autobiographical exposé of his lifelong battle to kick drug addictions and alcoholism, is a compelling account of a young and confused man fighting his demons, landing himself in one heap of trouble after another, culminating in a stint in jail.

However, there is only one problem with this incredible story. Apparently it was not completely true or, at the very least, significant details were changed. As book sales soared, pesky reporters who saw some flaws in Frey's story began to dig a little deeper and soon discovered that his account of reality did not correspond with the details of official records. Prodded by their critiques, Frey finally admitted he changed a few key aspects of his life. He insisted the majority of the book was true, a qualification that did not satisfy most of his critics.

Though his mishandling of the truth had journalists and readers up in arms, we should actually all have been thanking him for helping a nation of liars realize why we have such a problem telling the truth. Frey is an admitted addict, and addictions are fueled by a fear or refusal to accept reality or the truth out of weakness and/or selfishness, as Doug and Gail discussed; the addictions are a way of avoiding truth and running away from reality. So that Frey plays with the truth should not surprise us but it should enlighten us.

This is a nation rife with addictions to everything from alcohol, drugs, sex, and pornography to money, fame, and power. We don't just want these things; we are compulsively obsessed with them. Why are we addicted? Perhaps, it has to do with us being bombarded with bad news or with constant commercialism every day, aimed at convincing us that we are deprived and need more, better, and bigger everything: look as beautiful as those pretty people on TV, and surpass all expectations at our jobs, with our families, and with ourselves.

Then like the perfect pusher, our sensational society is there ready to offer us that escape in one of a hundred different opiates. We get hooked and then we must cover up that addiction with lies.

Like in the case of Frey, ultimately the truth always rises to the surface and rescues us—even from ourselves and actually because of our duplicity. Despite our addictions and deceit, sooner or later even the most deceitful of us tires of the isolation, secrecy, and loneliness that our lies and subsequent addictions produce. It is a relief when we get caught.

Essentially once everything that can go wrong has, then we become galvanized. It is not because we are immortal or superhuman but simply because we are strong and whole once we accept the true nature of our humanity—that we are animals with souls and conscience and an inbred desire to do the right thing and to care for each other. We are willing to see the lies that we have used to build a false fortress around our heart.

Once we are forced to open ourselves up to the truth, we are open to many other things as well. We are open to humility, to giving up the ego that demands that we live a certain way, that we have certain things that we want. We get past the need to be the center of our own universe, and we learn how to really practice the seven steps of serenity. It is not easy to be sure, and I am quite sure it takes a lifetime of constant work. The realization is more important than the achievement because once you see the world as one giant opportunity to love honestly, amazing things can happen.

So why would you look at that low point as a dead end? If everything that you have done or not done in your life has led you to suddenly realize that you need to change direction, that you are not going where you want to be, metaphysically speaking, then how could anyone logically call that a dead end? If our feelings of confusion, anger, fear, depression, or disorientation are signs of new birth, new ideas, and new experiences to come, then maybe it can inspire us to weather the storm. It is only a dead end if we are not opening our eyes and seeing the greatest road map to enlightenment and elation in the world.

Losing Your Freedom and Finding Your Soul

Two young professional women, one in Phoenix and one in Dallas, Alexis and Robin, never met each other. They came from different backgrounds and places and faced very similar ordeals at the same time. They both ended up better off for it.

Alexis could talk her way in or out of just about any situation. The thirty-eight-year-old former pageant queen was deceptive in her communication skills, everything from her age to even her identity to get a better deal or a better room at a hotel or a ticket to an invitation-only social event, or even a new job. Plain and simple, Alexis lied repeatedly. She would tell one lie to her family, another to her employer, another to her friends. *"I thought I was the only one I could trust,"* said Alexis. *"I believed that all successful people thought like that. If anyone knew your secrets or what you were vulnerable to then eventually they would use that to hurt you and to destroy you."* Regardless of what experiences may have made her think that way in the first place, eventually it resulted in one heck of a self-fulfilling prophecy. Her attitude attracted exactly the kind of behavior she feared from family to boyfriends to employers. That hardened her heart and her resolve even more to distance herself from anyone and from the truth. *"All I needed was financial security,"* said Alexis. *"If I had that I wouldn't need anything or anyone else."*

Nobody ever knew the real Alexis, including Alexis. At the end of the day, she was usually clever enough that she could get out of whatever situation in which she found herself. She finally went too far. After taking a job managing a high-profile, high-end jewelry boutique in Dallas, she found herself in the best and worst possible place for someone of dubious character teetering on the edge of a breakdown.

Alexis figured she could get away with a little blurring of the inventory lists. Before long she had doubled sales, and items were flying out of the store. The only problem was nobody was actually paying for them. *"It was absolute insanity,"* said Alexis. *"I didn't know what was real anymore. I convinced myself I was above it all. But I was ready to explode inside because of all the lies and the fear of getting caught."*

One thing was for sure. She was not getting away with it. It was just a matter of time before her lies and the balance sheet caught up with her. That is the day a local police detective called, and a few days later she found herself the best-dressed debutante in the country lockup, charged with grand theft and facing three years in jail.

While Alexis was in jail, a few states away in Arizona, Robin was leaving a local bar and grill after having a few too many drinks. She was a hard-working professional woman with her share of stress, who was inclined to deal with it by drinking. The thirty-four-year-old wife and mother of two young children was by no means an alcoholic, but she was not exactly a card-carrying member of the Ladies Temperance League either, and on this particular night she had a few too many. *"I hadn't had anything to eat for dinner and I'd been drinking pretty steadily for about five hours,"* admitted Robin. *"Obviously I had no business driving that night, but of course I thought I was fine."*

Robin climbed behind the wheel of her SUV certain that she was sober enough to make it home safely, but she did not even make it out of the parking lot when she plowed right into someone. Robin was uninjured, but the woman she hit broke her leg, and her car was demolished. Robin was arrested, and a blood test at the police station showed her blood alcohol level over the legal limit. After a few hours in a jail cell, she was released into a friend's custody without being charged. She thought that was the end of it. *"I figured I would be charged with drunk driving,"* said Robin. *"I hired a lawyer to get the police report, but I still didn't think it was a big deal."*

However, nine months later, Robin received a heart-stopping letter in the mail. She was being indicted for aggravated assault with a weapon, the official charge brought against anyone who causes an injury to another while driving impaired. It was a serious criminal offense, carrying with it a mandatory prison term that no judge could excuse. She was facing up to seven years in jail. To complicate matters, her insurance company dropped her,

her license was suspended, and the woman was suing her for half-a-million dollars. *"I was terrified,"* confided Robin. *"Overnight I went from a law-abiding citizen to a felon."*

Robin went to her boss, explained the situation, and begged for his help and understanding. He referred her to a high-profile attorney. Even the best lawyer in town could not get her out of this spot. *"He worked out a deal where I would spend one year in Tent City on work release,"* explained Robin. *"I would go in every day after work, sleep in jail, and then leave in the morning for work."* Arizona's infamous Tent City was run by no-nonsense Sheriff Joe Arpaio. It was an outdoor facility in the middle of the desert outside of Phoenix where average temperatures soared into the triple digits in the summer with only fans to cool the inmates, not to mention stale food and cramped quarters.

Before checking into jail, Robin wrote letters to everyone at work explaining to them what happened and admitting to her crime. *"Some of those people were very supportive,"* said Robin. *"Others told me I deserved what I got, and they were right. I drove drunk, and I could have killed that woman."* She made arrangements for her children to stay with her parents for a year while she and her husband faced this situation.

Meanwhile back in Dallas, Alexis finally came to terms with a life of lies while sitting in a jail cell waiting to get bailed out. *"That was the most humiliating, lowest point in my life,"* said Alexis. *"I was surrounded by drug addicts and hookers. But I couldn't pretend I was any better than they were anymore. This was real, and there was no lying my way out of it. I spent my whole life running away from people who I thought could hurt me. But there was no running now. I couldn't even walk out the door."*

It took Alexis a lot of honesty and a lot of money, neither of which she had much of, to get herself out of hot water. She had to pay back all the money she took with interest, plus about as much in legal fees and fines, all of which she had to borrow. In order to find someone she could trust to represent her, she had to expose herself and her crime to friends and family. *"I had to humble myself to a lot of people,"* confided Alexis. *"And I had to come clean about a lot of other things too. I lost everything—my self-esteem, my self-confidence, and a whole lot of money."*

Back in Phoenix, Robin was ready to pay her dues. When she got to court, her attorney informed her she would be eligible for house arrest in six months. Then when the judge signed the order, by some miracle, she wrote that she would be immediately eligible. *"My lawyer still doesn't understand why she did that,"* said Robin. *"But just like that I had my life back."* She still had to endure four days in the tents while paperwork was processed, but then she was released into house arrest, which allowed her to go to work, as long as she alerted a probation officer by pager of her every move.

Robin worked to rebuild her life over the next ten years. *"It made me realize I needed to take life and my actions a little more seriously,"* said Robin. *"It made me realize how important my children were to me. After that my job didn't seem as important as the people I worked with. I didn't worry so much about how I looked or how much we had. It brought me and my husband closer together than ever."* That closeness with her husband came to be a priceless experience when he unexpectedly died less than three years later of brain cancer.

Other things started to make sense as well. She found out that the woman she sent to the hospital had sent a letter to the judge asking that she not be sent to jail. Robin also ran into the judge that had given her leniency sitting behind her in church one day when she turned around to offer the sign of peace.

As part of her plea arrangement, she agreed to do community service at her church, working with teenagers and helping them to stay away from drugs and alcohol. *"It cost me $25,000 in legal fees and fines, but if I have stopped one teenager from getting hurt or hurting someone else it was worth it,"* said Robin. *"And now I'm like a broken record telling people not to drink and drive. Maybe I made a difference with somebody."*

Without a criminal record and thanks to another under-standing judge who was willing to give her one chance to straighten up and fly right, Alexis got off on probation as well, and she decided to spend a little bit of her newfound life helping children too. She went to local media organizations and was finally able to convince one of the TV networks to begin a series of sponsored fund-raising events to help awareness and treatment of wayward teens. *"When my life came to a crashing halt the way it did, I thought about all the reasons why it could have happened. I had to rebuild it from the ground up. Now I'm not afraid anymore of anything or anyone, or concerned with what anybody thinks about me. I used to live in a state of fear. I wanted to be in control of everything before, but I was actually totally out of control. Now I accept what comes my way, and I'm more stable than ever. It makes it a lot easier to love people."*

The Priest Story

When I was in elementary school, a priest came to visit my Catholic school to tell us a story of why and how he became a priest. I was expecting some "holy mission from God" story aimed at recruiting future priests, but what I heard was very dif-ferent. He told us of a young and confused man who was jilted by his girlfriend and wound up on a bridge one cold and rainy night, ready to jump.

This was not some unreal story of a life gone wrong that I heard about on TV or in the newspapers. It was a real man standing in front of me, telling me his all-too-real story of a human being who was ready to give up because he had concluded that he was just not worthy of living. Yet here he was several decades later very much alive and brimming with all the joy, purpose, and meaning in his life that we all seek.

Besides being riveting enough to hold the attention of a pre-pubescent youth growing up on video games and cable TV, the priest's dramatic story was a milestone for me. It was one of the first times I heard somebody I knew talk so candidly about life, death, and the feelings of despair that we all have at some point in our lives whether we admit it or not. I think it had a great deal to do with why today I can look at such despair with such a positive attitude.

The priest explained that he had no reason to live if the love of his life was not there for him. While sitting up there on that dark and lonely bridge in the cold for hours he ruminated over and over again in his mind: Why did she not want him? Why was he not good enough? Why was he so empty? Why bother to go on every day in pain and anguish? What was the point of life?

That is when it hit him. He spent his whole life avoiding answering those questions but he needed to answer them. We all need to answer them. Now because he lost what he thought was everything, he was up on a bridge asking these questions. He realized in a flash that this was not the end but "the end of the beginning," to borrow another phrase from the great politician and British prime minister Winston Churchill.

He did not know the answers to any of those questions at that point but the realization that he was summoned to answer to them was enough to get him off that bridge. He decided he needed to keep on living for as long as it took him to find those answers, and he is still fervently searching for that wisdom by helping so many others find their way.

His despair was not imagined. It was real and it woke him up to a stark reality that something was missing in his life. He went on to help so many people because of it, including me when I had problems in school, my family, and many close friends of mine.

He has undoubtedly helped many more people deal with just about every catastrophe mentioned in this book. It was all made possible because he once faced the greatest hardship of them all—the desire to give up on living.

Second Chances

People say that we do not get a second chance in life, but I disagree. I think God in his almighty wisdom provides second chances, as well as third, fourth, and more chances than we can count to figure out how to live the life he wants us to lead.

Sometimes we just keep on throwing away our second chances. However, every day of our lives, we all get another chance. We can stop and say hello instead of rushing around like a self-obsessed egomaniac trying to make a buck. We can call our parents in the middle of a busy day just to say we love them and appreciate everything they ever did for us, even though they might not have done everything right when rearing us. We can find a smile and a kind word for our neighbor, even while in the clouds of confusion that invade our heart when we lose those we love. We can apologize to someone we have wronged in the past. We can stop hurting ourselves through addictions and other self-abusive behaviors and learn how to help others do the same, and we can stop hurting others through belligerent or rambunctious behavior, regardless of the reason.

We can see the sunrise or feel the rain caress our skin, and we can make that experience even better for others through our appreciation and perception of it. We can thank God for that second chance by making the world and ourselves better, stronger, and lovelier with every hardship, so that everyone else will have a second chance to put their past mistakes, misfortune, and hardship behind them and to plot a course toward peace, prosperity, and reconciliation.

We all have a second chance to make peace, love, and respect for God and the world that he gave us the goal of our reign here on Earth.

So next time you are tempted to let despair dominate your day, convinced you are too mired in your own mistakes or misfortune to rebound, remember that Christ died not just so you could overcome death after life, but so you could also defeat the death of depression that earthly demons shall tempt you to succumb to every day.

Consider that as you celebrate life, and do not become overwhelmed by your own imperfection, your misfortune, or the temporal unhappiness that all too often greets us in this world. Instead, be a joyful servant of the Lord's powerful potential of life's most common catastrophes.

Notes

Chapter 1

- Opening quotation is from Viktor E. Frankl, *Man's Search for Meaning* (New York: Pocket Books, 1963), 104.
1. Frankl, 116.

Chapter 4

1. "Jessica Simpson Saw Therapist Over Rumors," *AP Online* (11 November 2005).
2. Michelle Archer, "Founder of Patagonia Became a Businessman Accidentally," *USA Today* (31 October 2005):5B.
3. Lisa M. Krieger, "Apple CEO Challenges Stanford Graduates," *San Jose Mercury News* (13 June 2005):1B.
4. Interview: Michael Finkel, *Morning Edition* on NPR (2 June 2005).
5. Ken Leiser, "20 Years After Strike, Fired Controller Is Back in the Tower at Lambert Field," *St. Louis Post-Dispatch* (29 July 2001):D3.
6. P. B. Gray and Dory Devlin, "Heroes of Small Business," *Fortune Small Business Magazine* (1 November 2000).

7. Patricia Sellers, "So You Fail. Now Bounce Back." *Fortune* (1 May 1995) Cover Story.

8. Marilyn Gardner, "Laid Off at 50," *Christian Science Monitor* (7 February 2005).

9. Bill Breen, "Starting Over...and Over," *Fast Company* (1 January 2002):74.

Chapter 5

1. Mary Jordan and Kevin Sullivan, *The Prison Angel: Mother Antonia's Journey from Beverly Hills to a Life of Service in a Mexican Jail* (New York: Penguin Press, 2005).

Chapter 7

1. James Dao, "Instant Millions Can't Halt Winners' Grim Slide," *New York Times* (5 December 2005):A-1.

2. Ibid.

3. Janine DeFao, "Hurricane Katrina: Bay Area Response," *San Francisco Chronicle* (11 September 2005):A-23.

4. Andy Hirsch, "Katrina Victims Settle in Snyder County, broadcast on WNEP (19 December 2005).

5. Blake Bailey "My Year of Hurricanes—I lost everything in Katrina." *Slate* Online Magazine (2 September 2005).

Chapter 9

1. Statement read by Suzanne Vitadamo and Bobby Schindler, Woodside Hospice, Pinellas Park, FL (31 March 2005).